Cute, Adorable Cats and Kittens

A Grayscale Coloring Book

Ashley Blackman

ISBN-13: 978-1532766428
ISBN-10: 1532766424

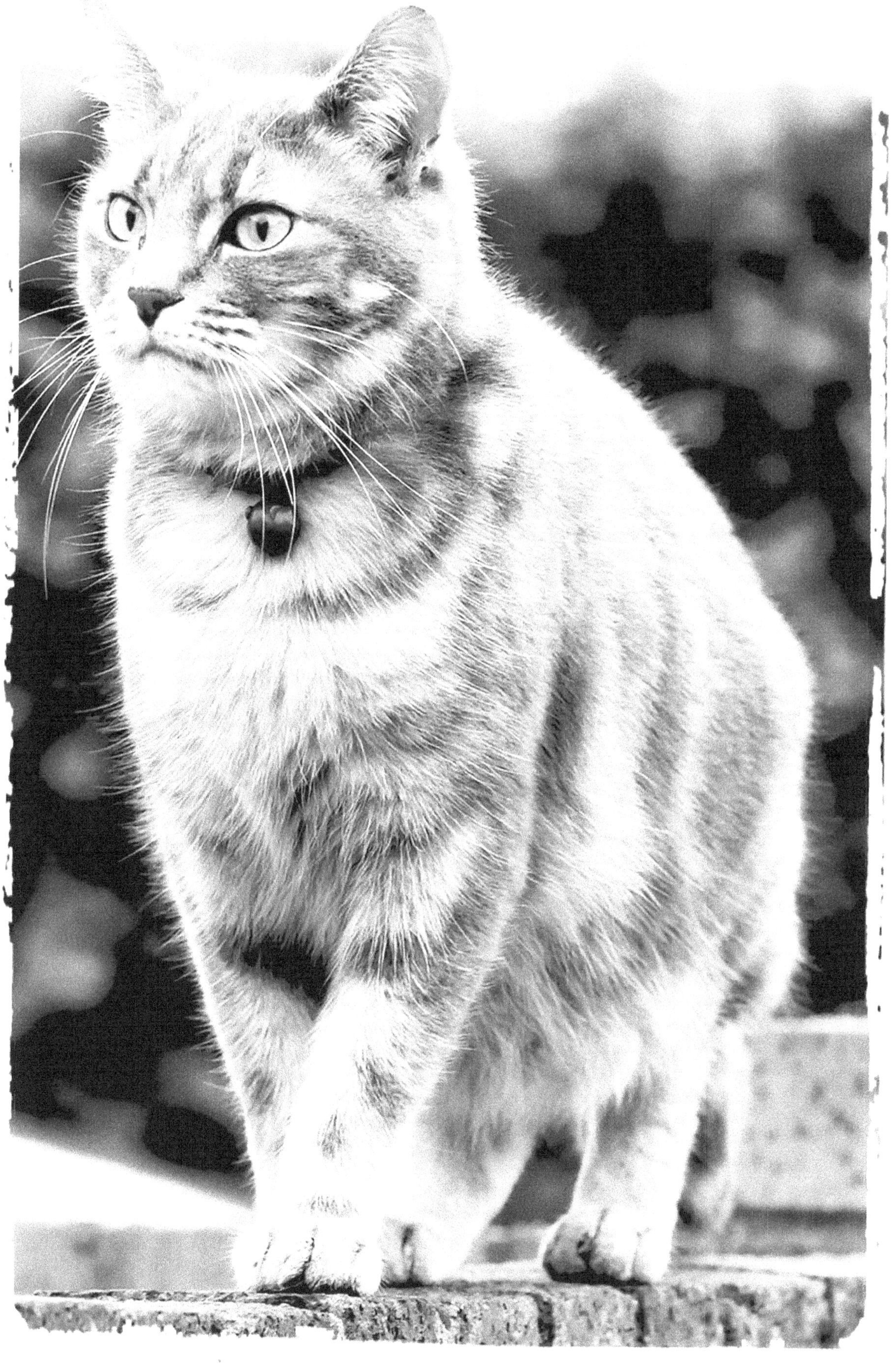

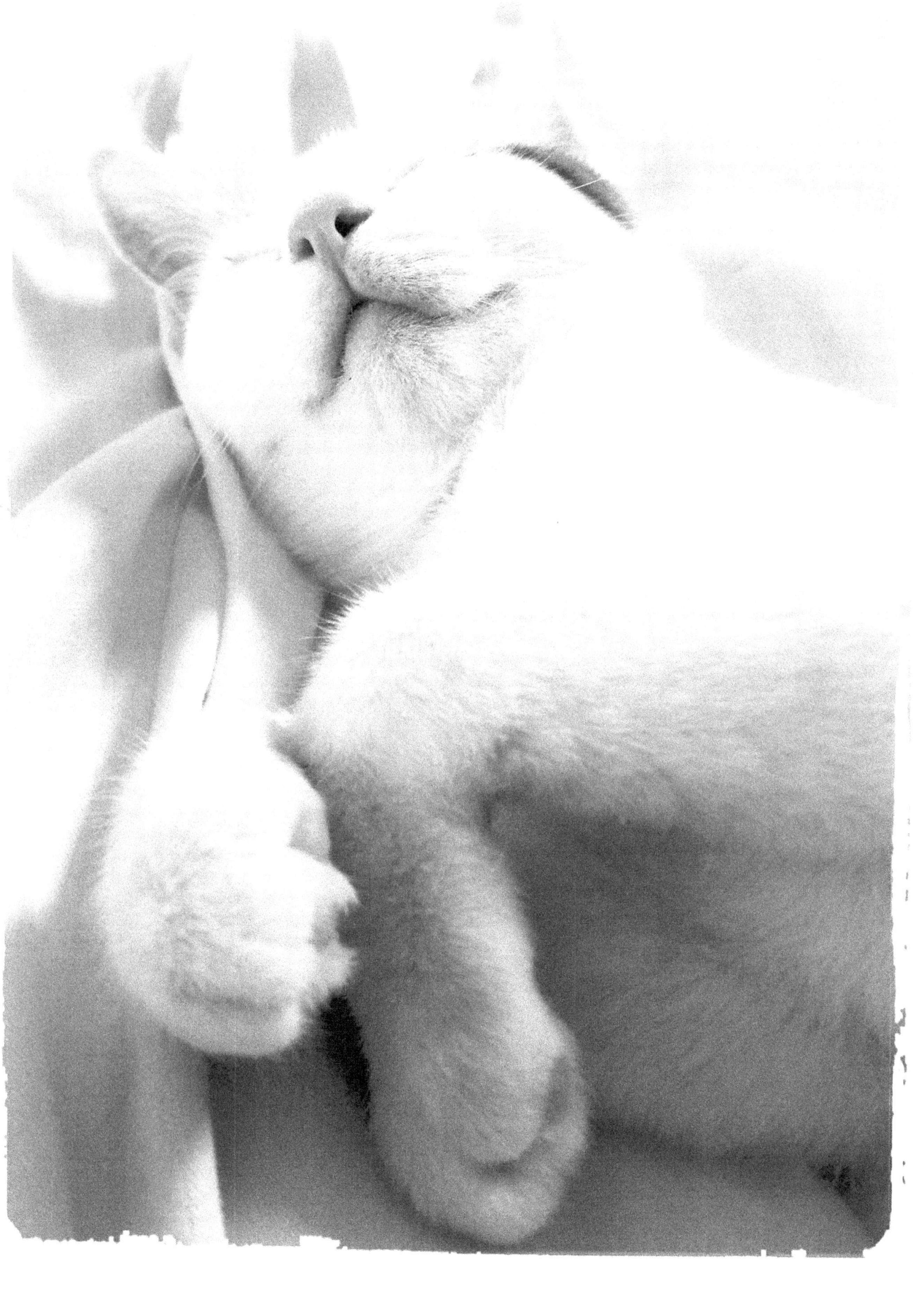

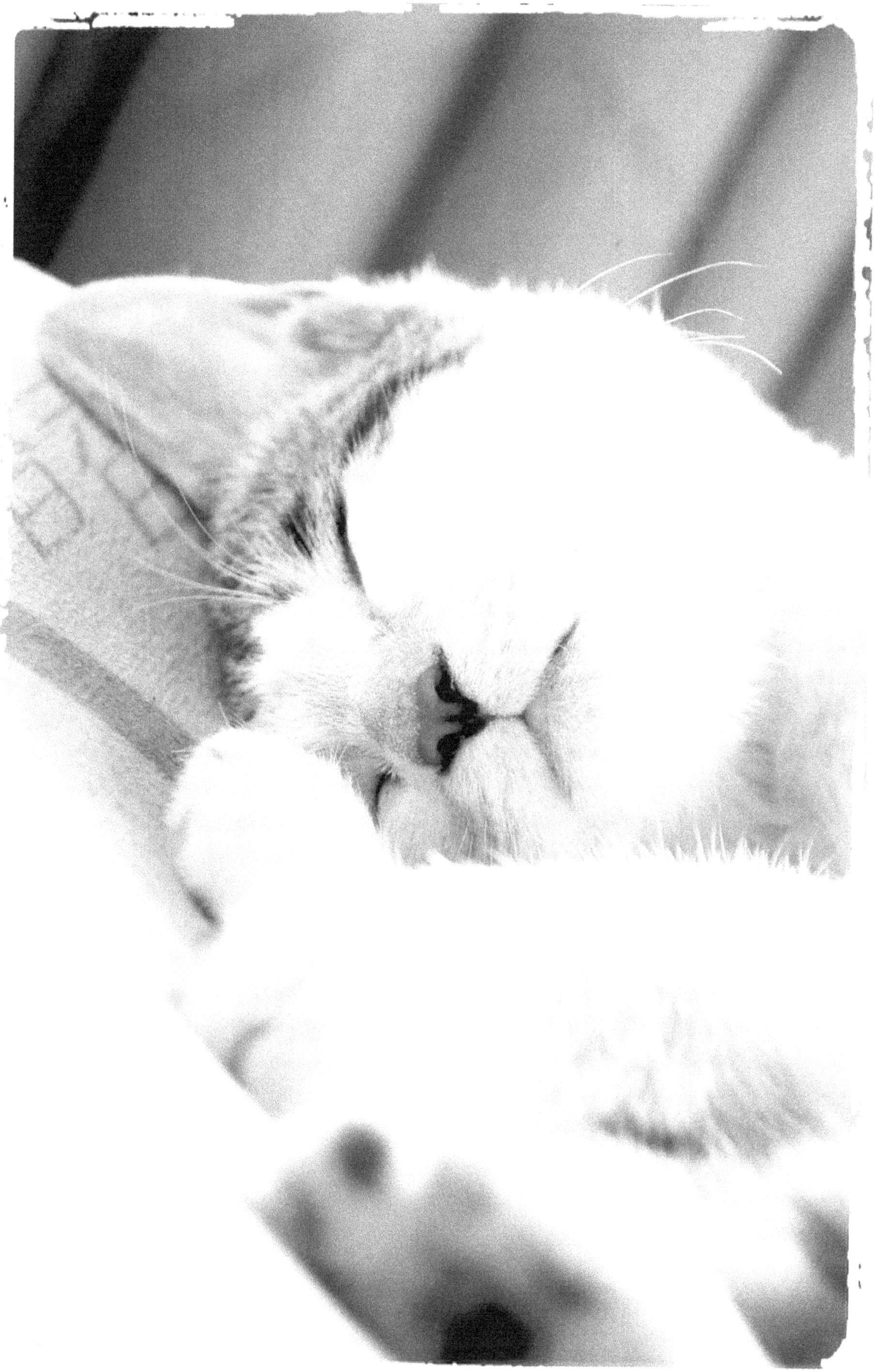

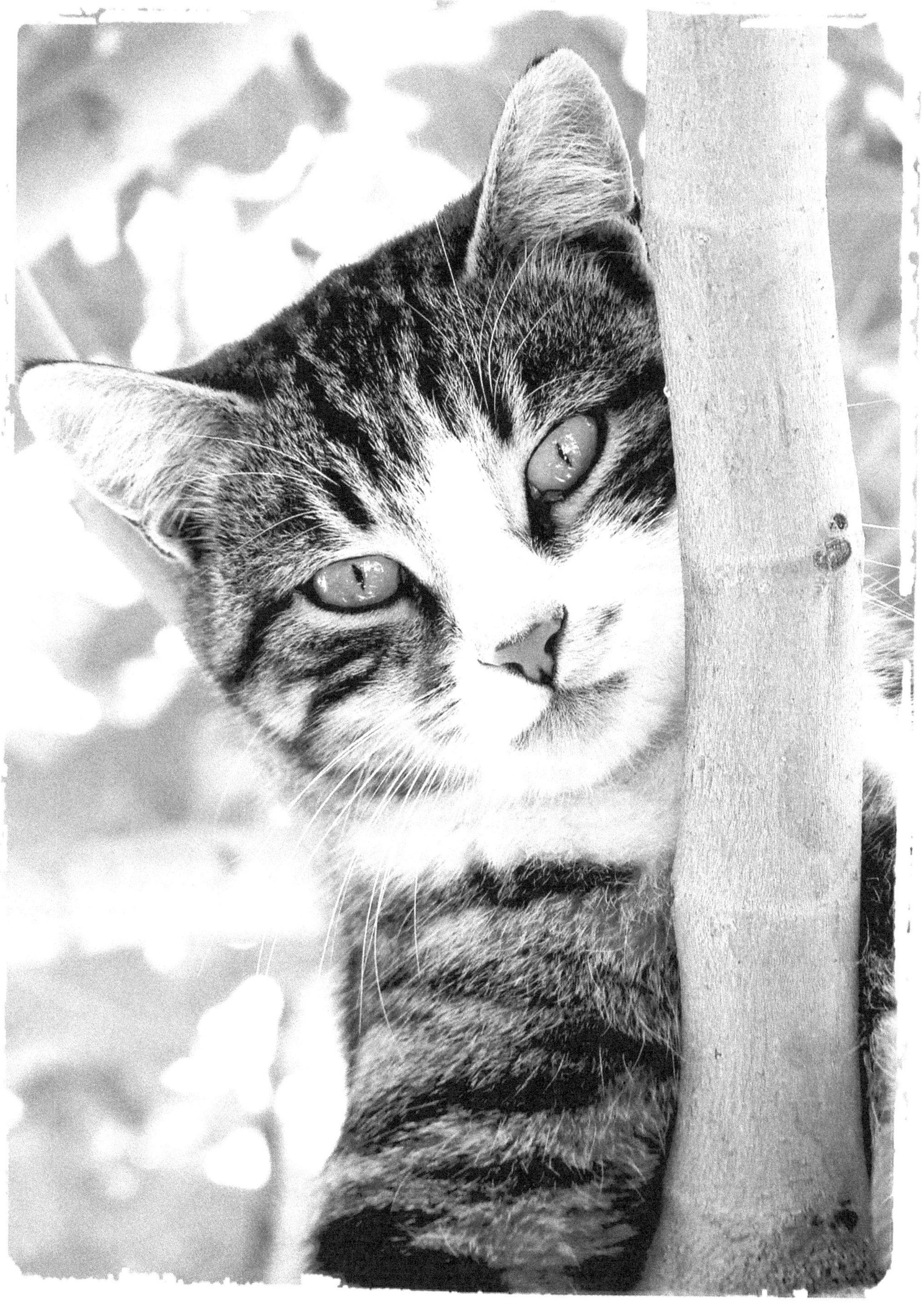

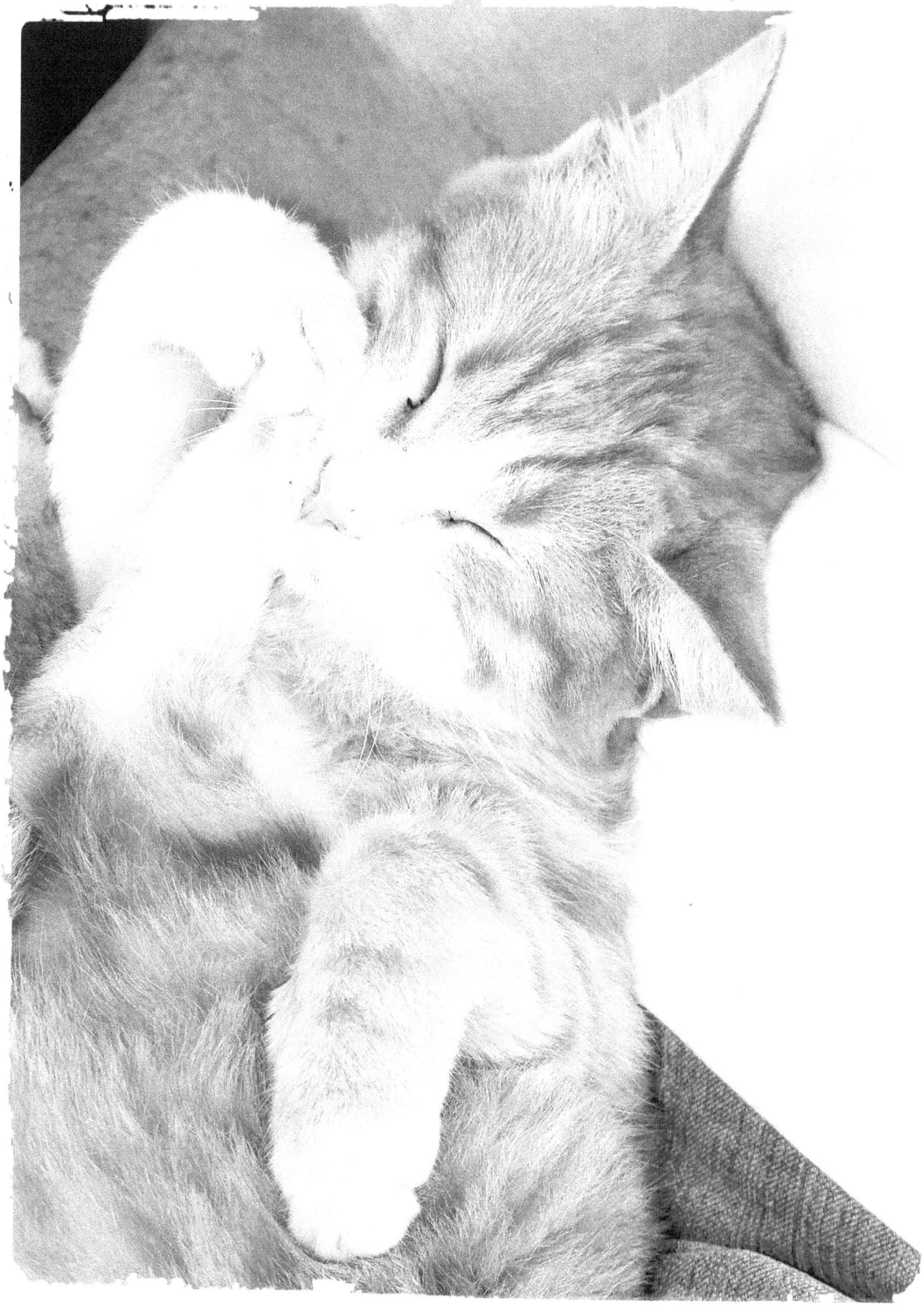

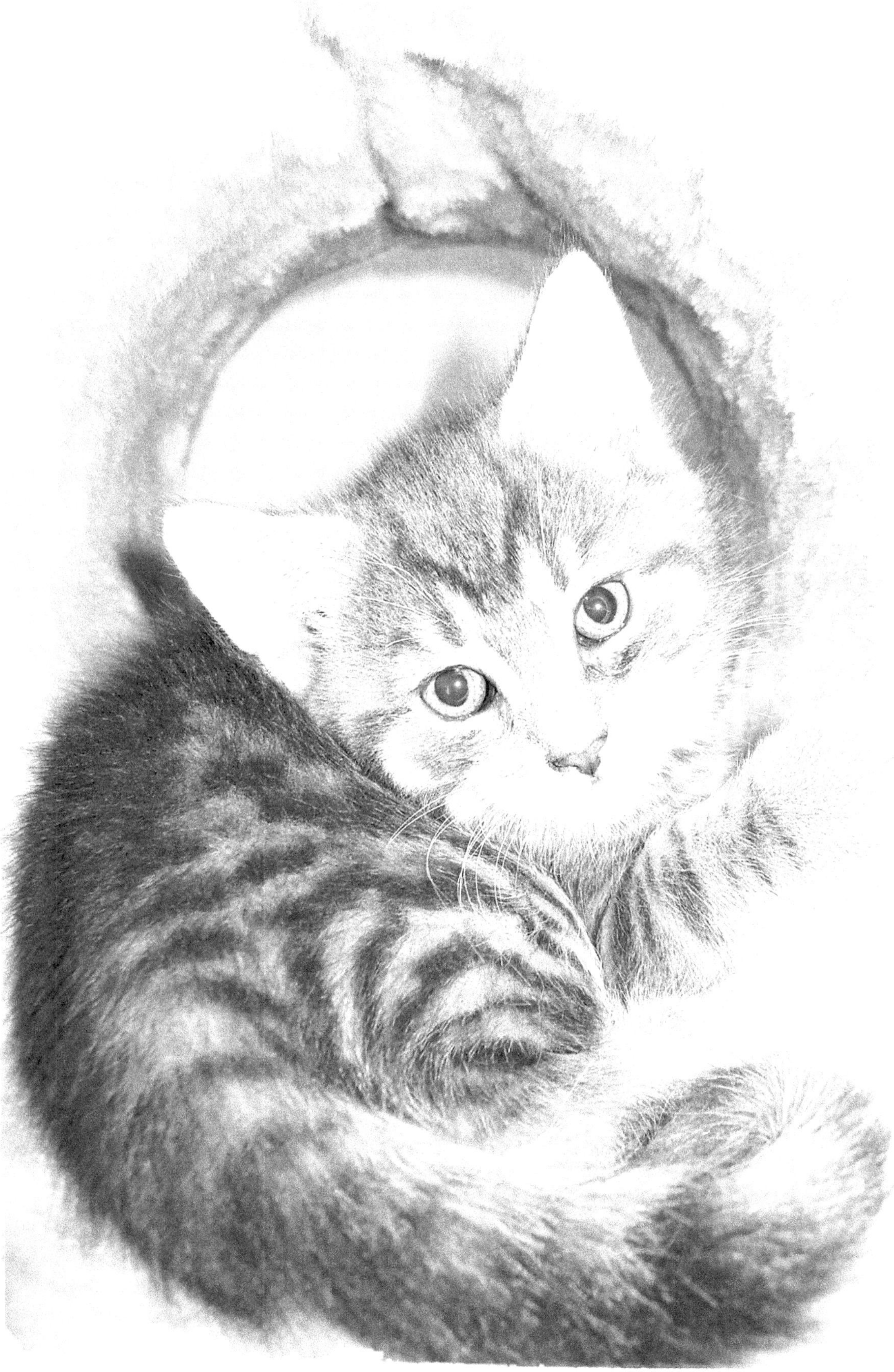

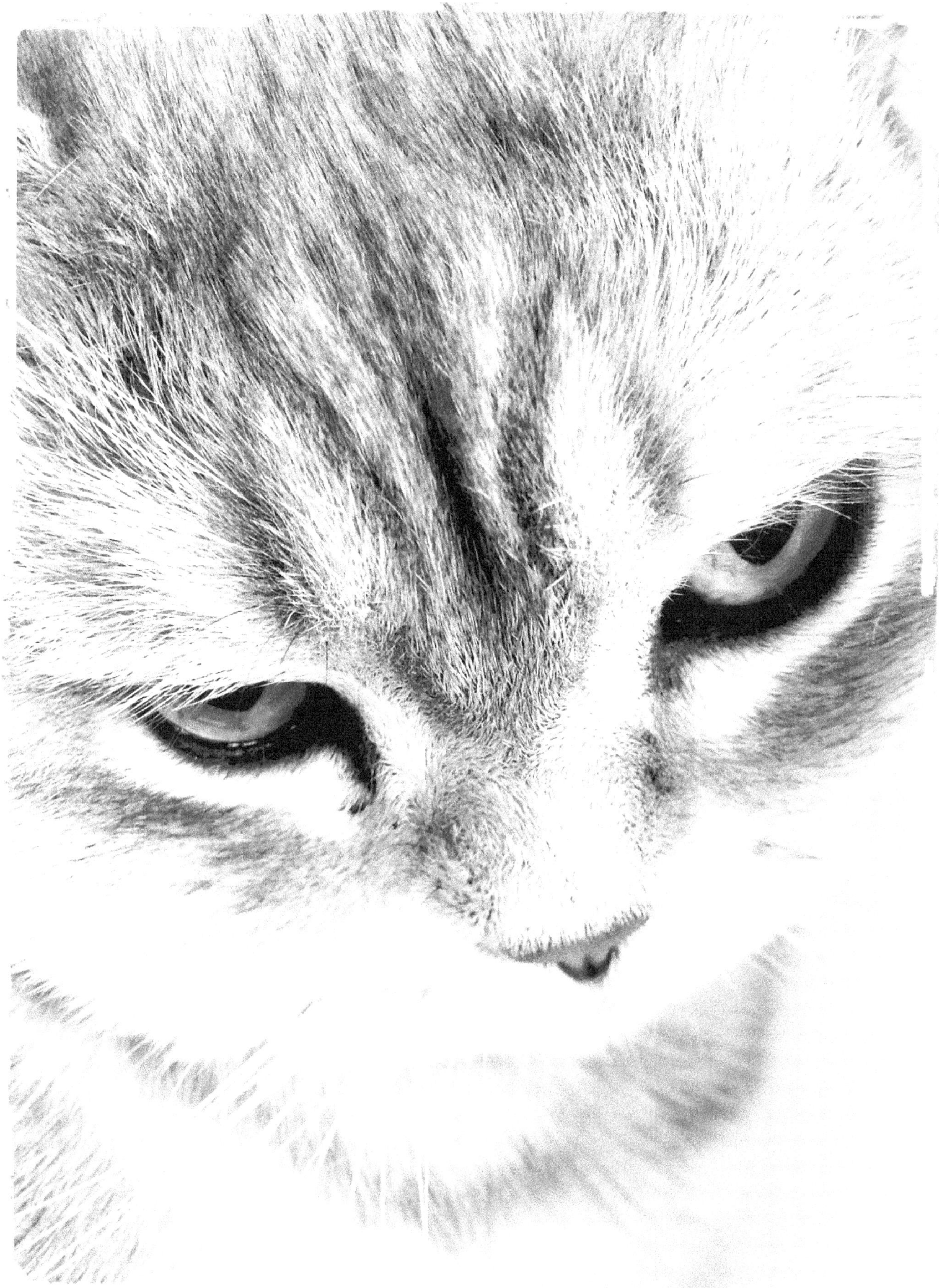

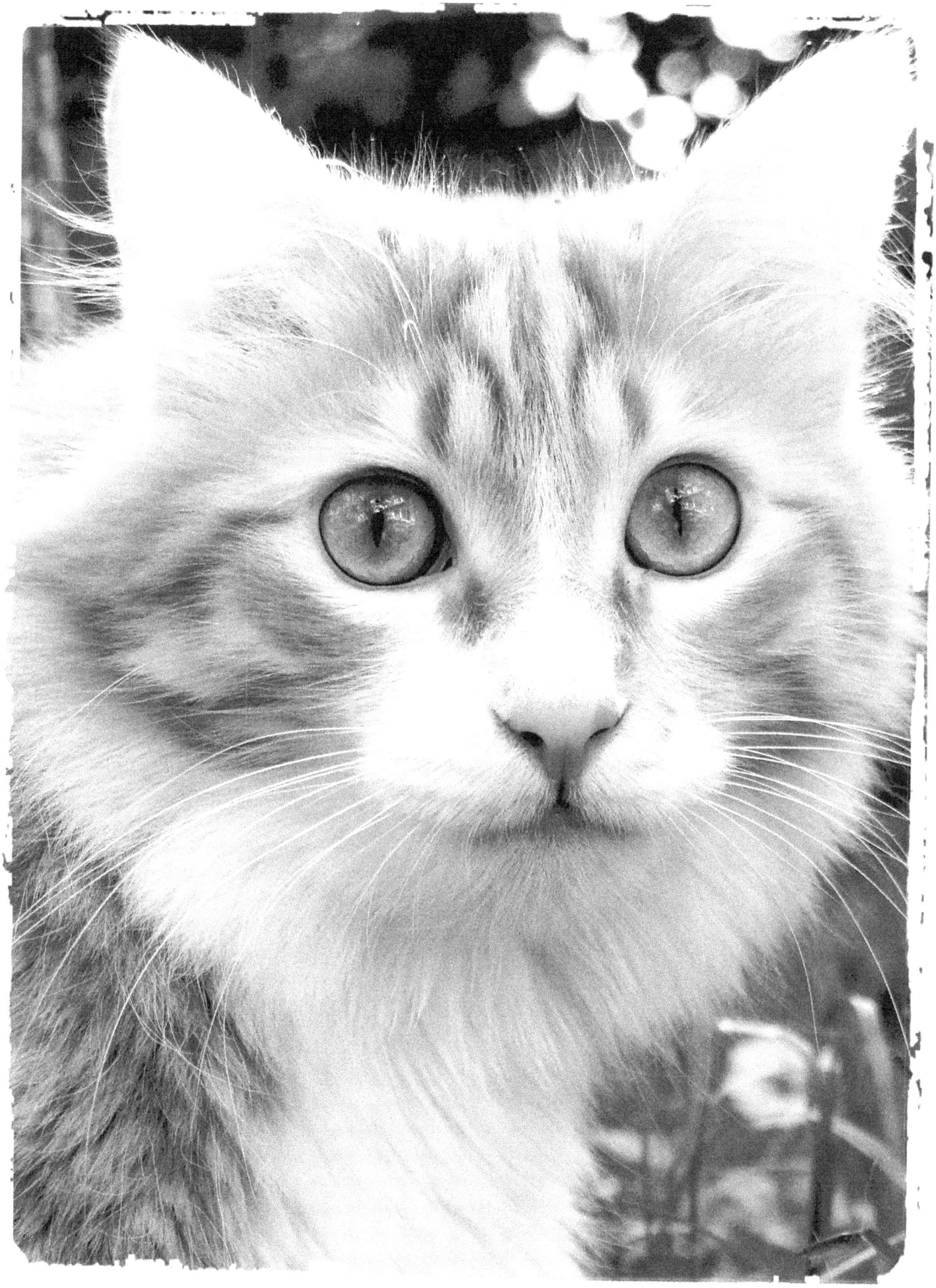

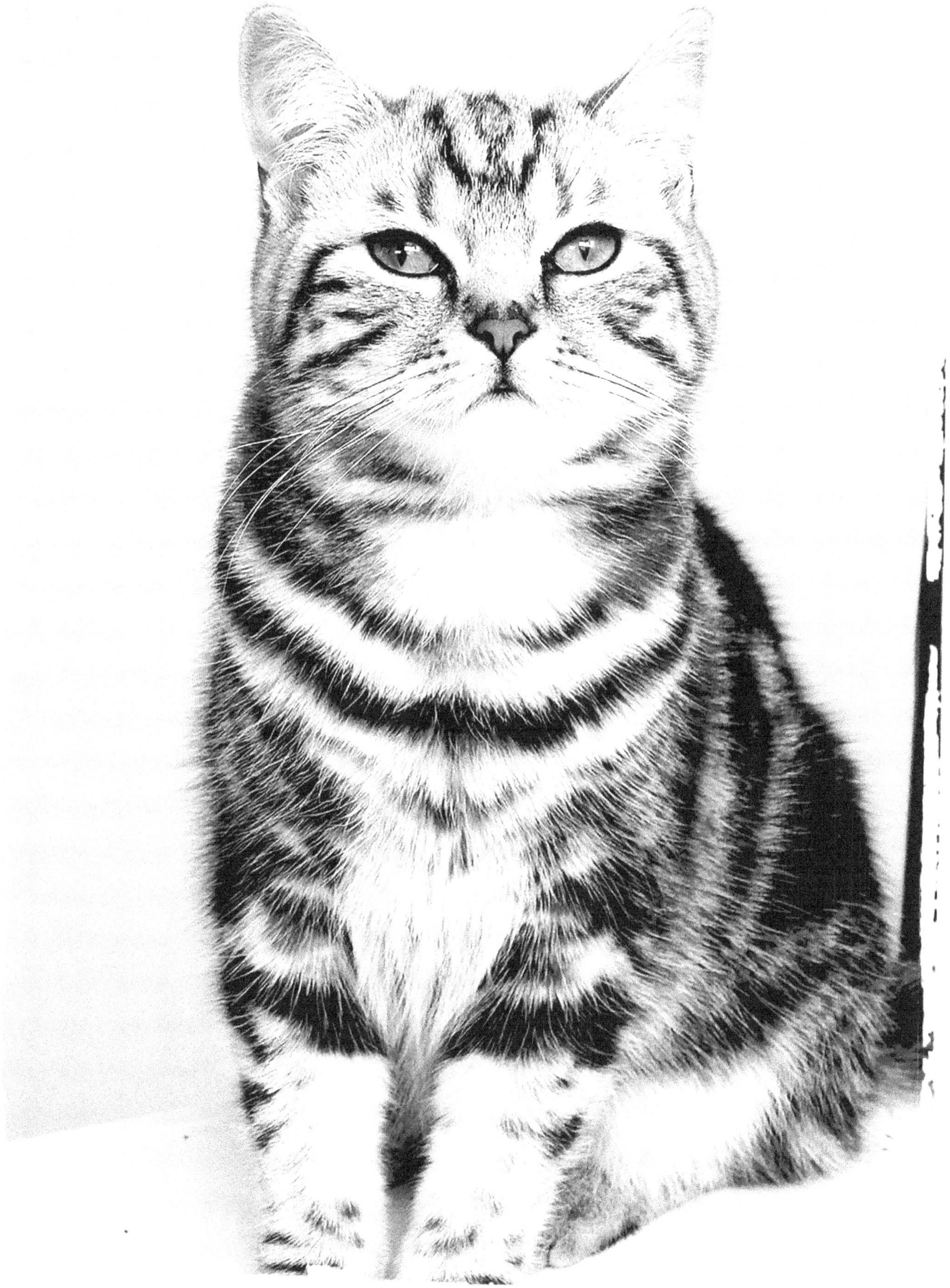

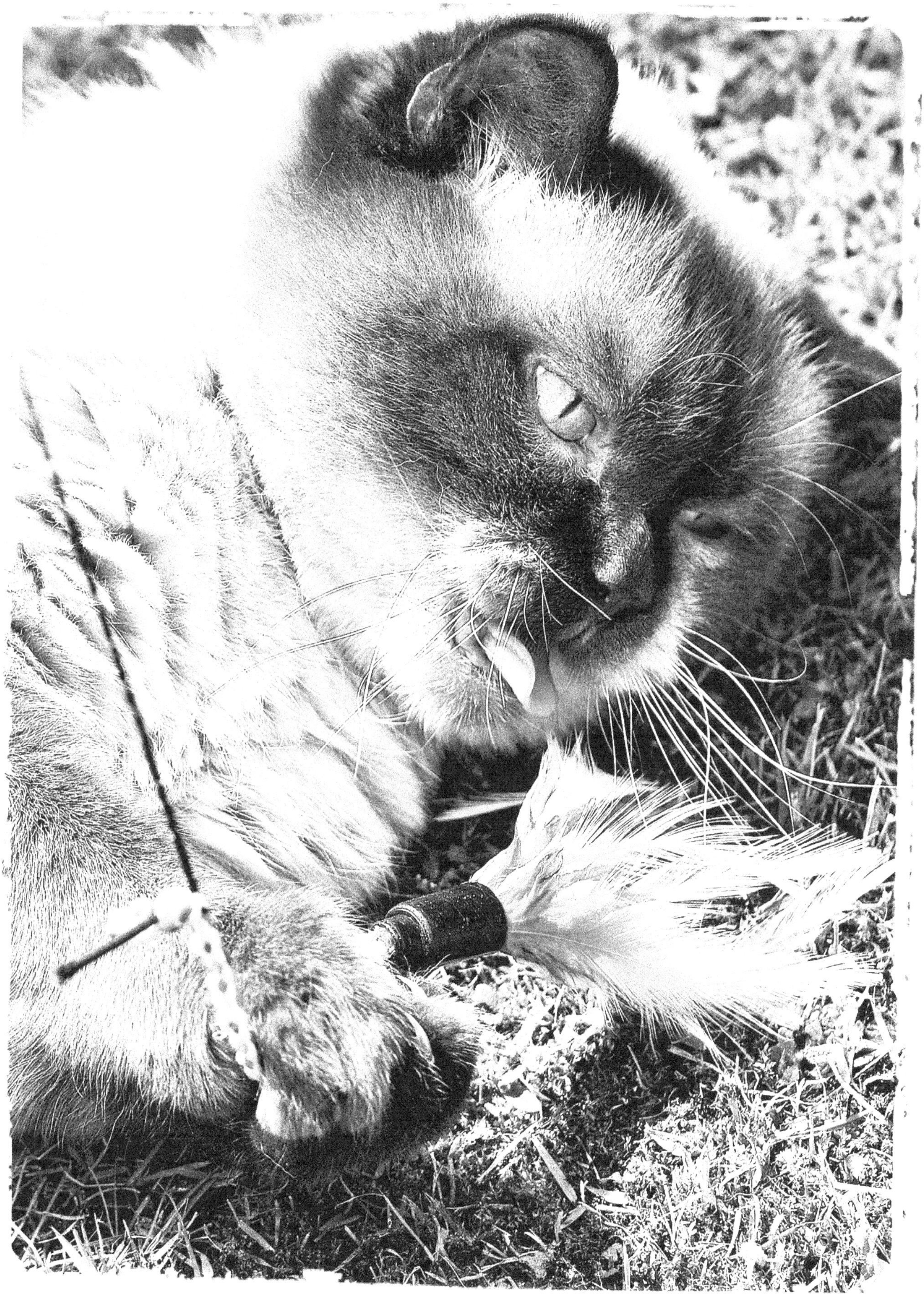

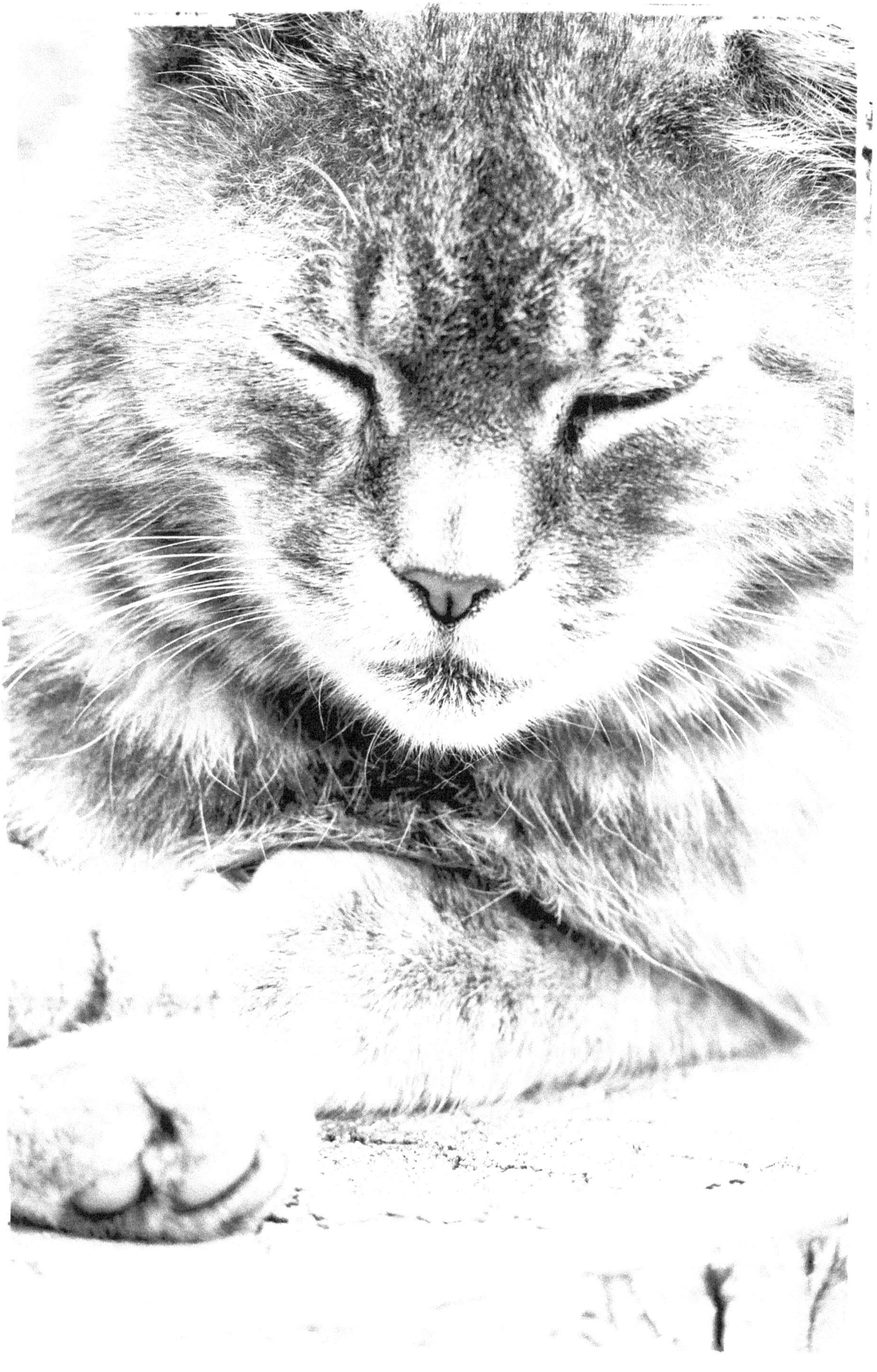

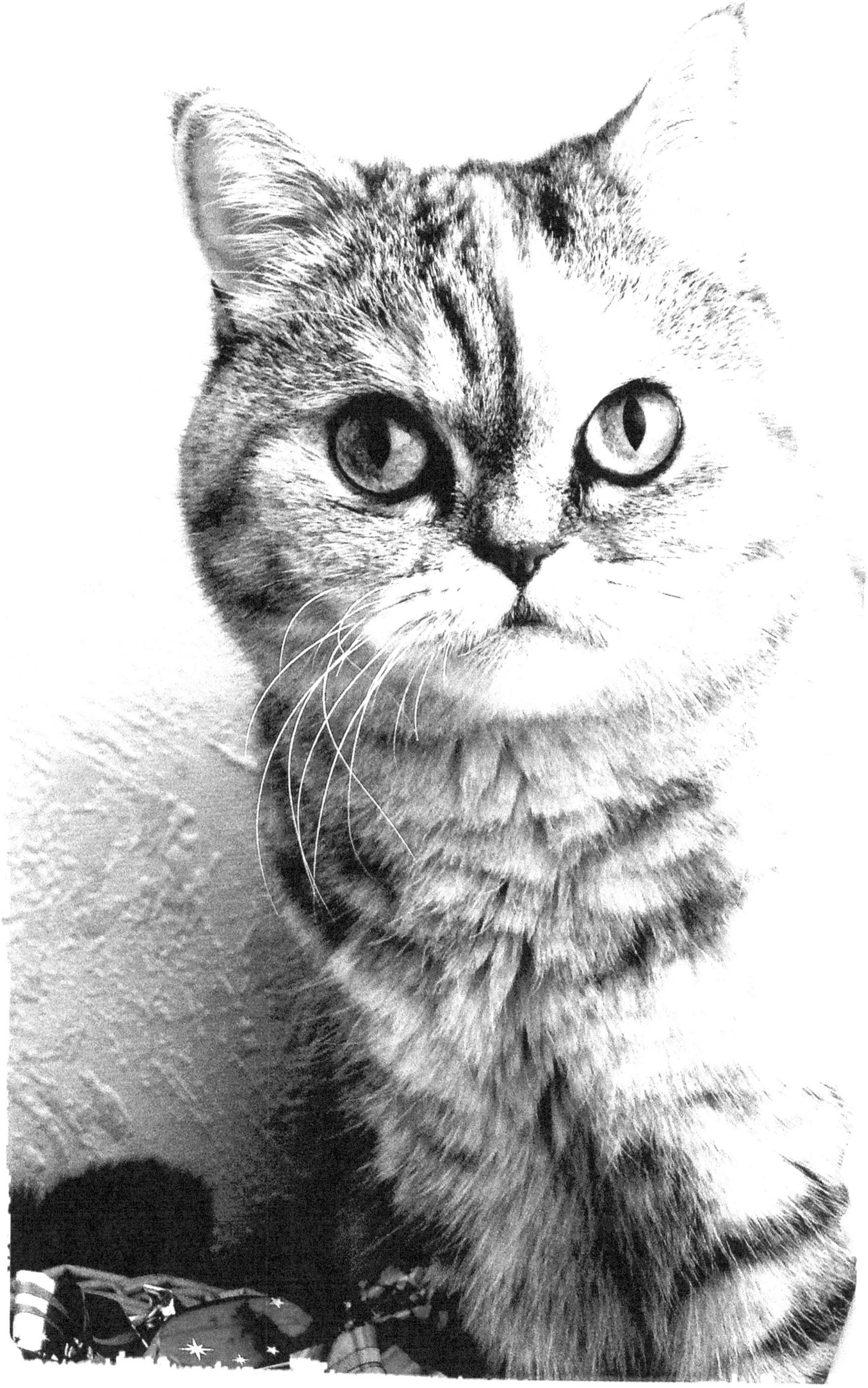

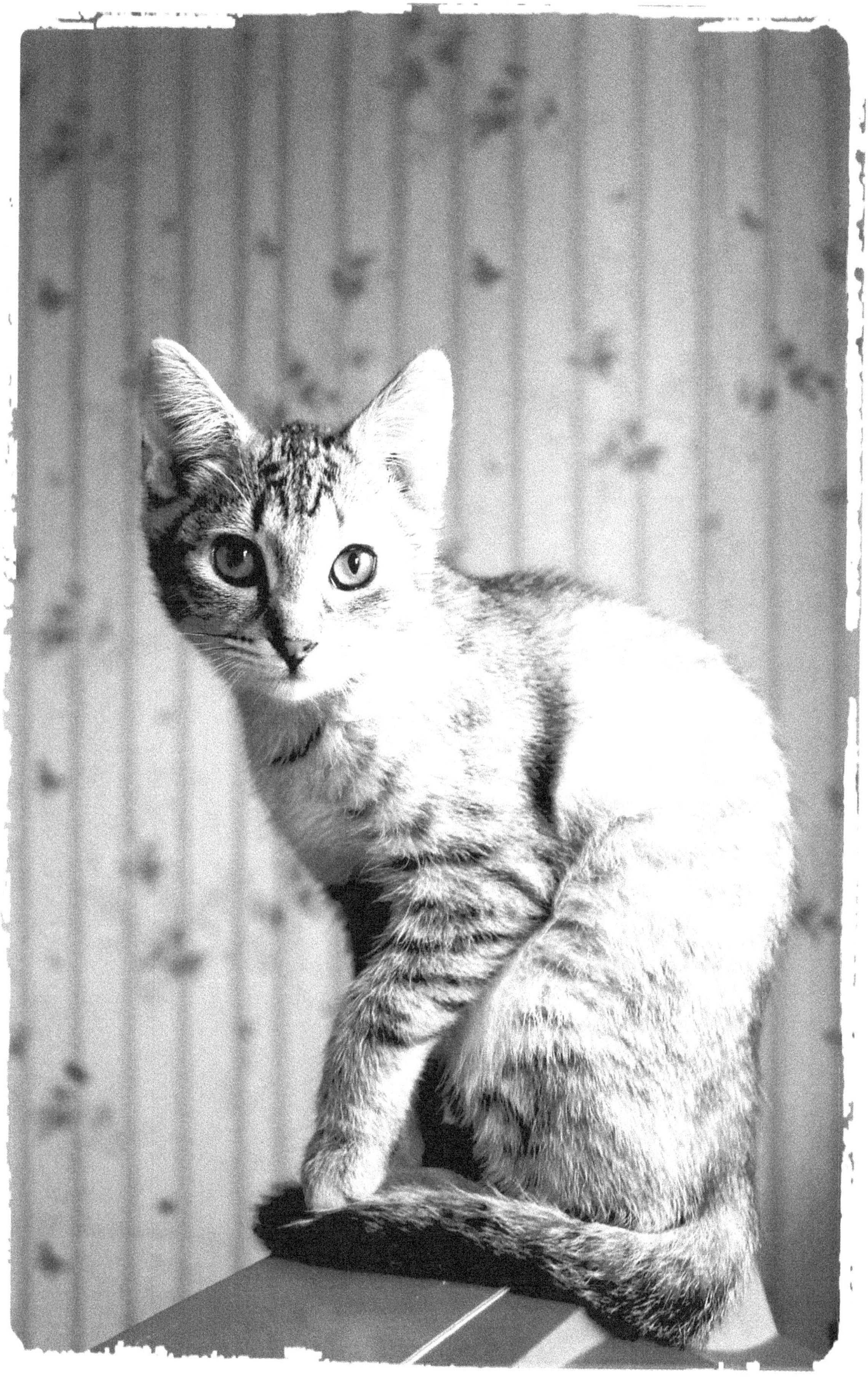

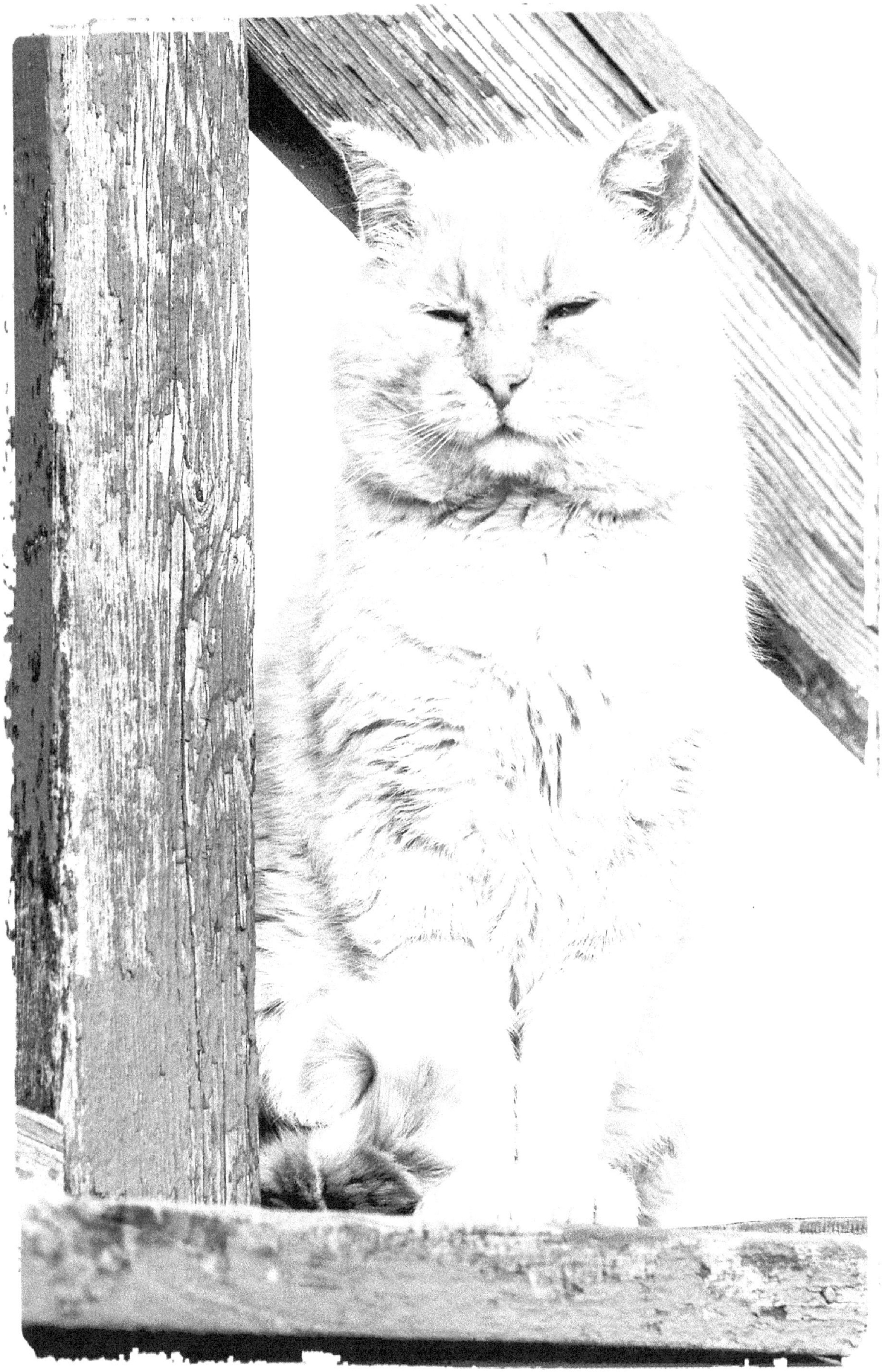

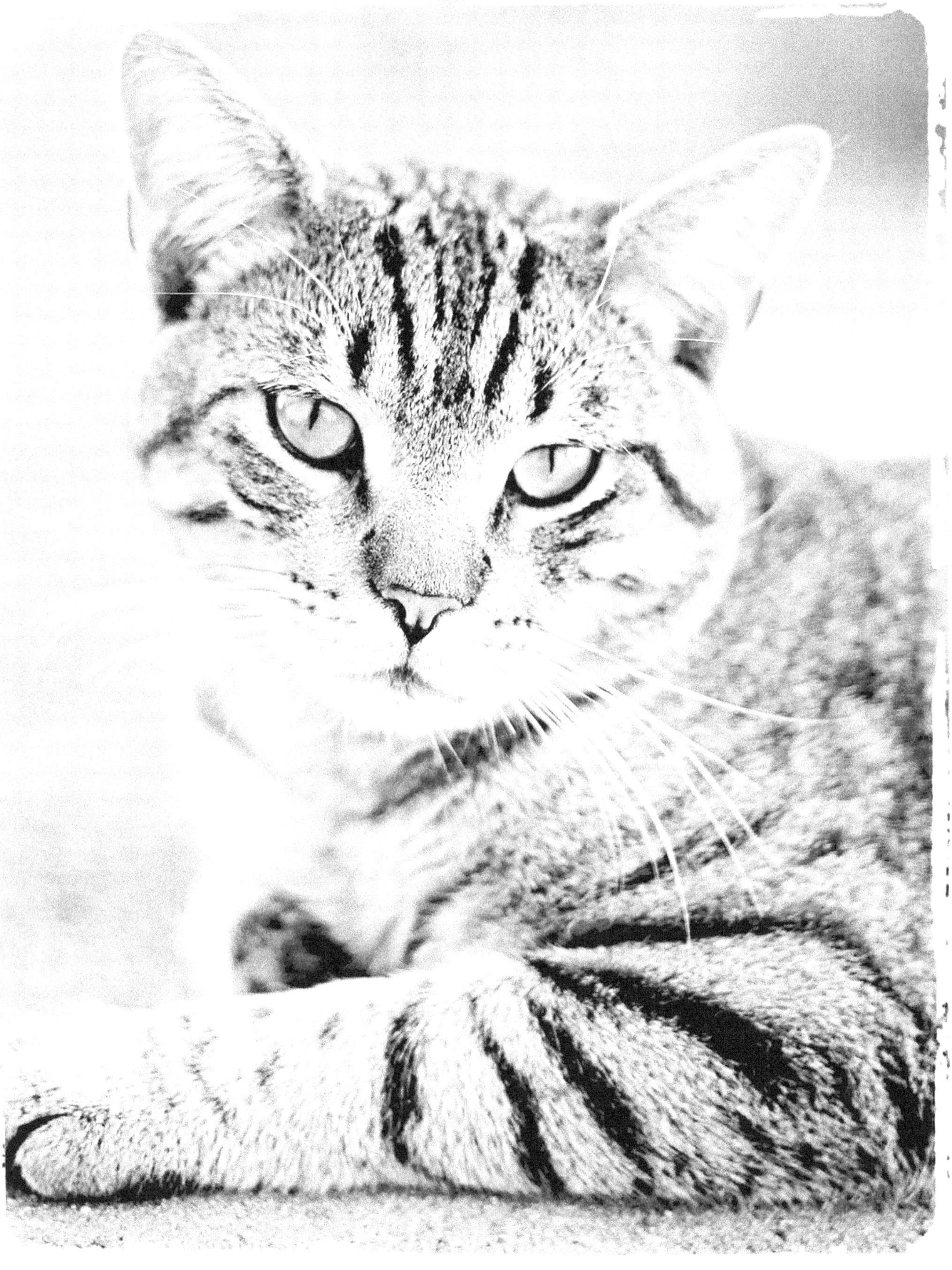

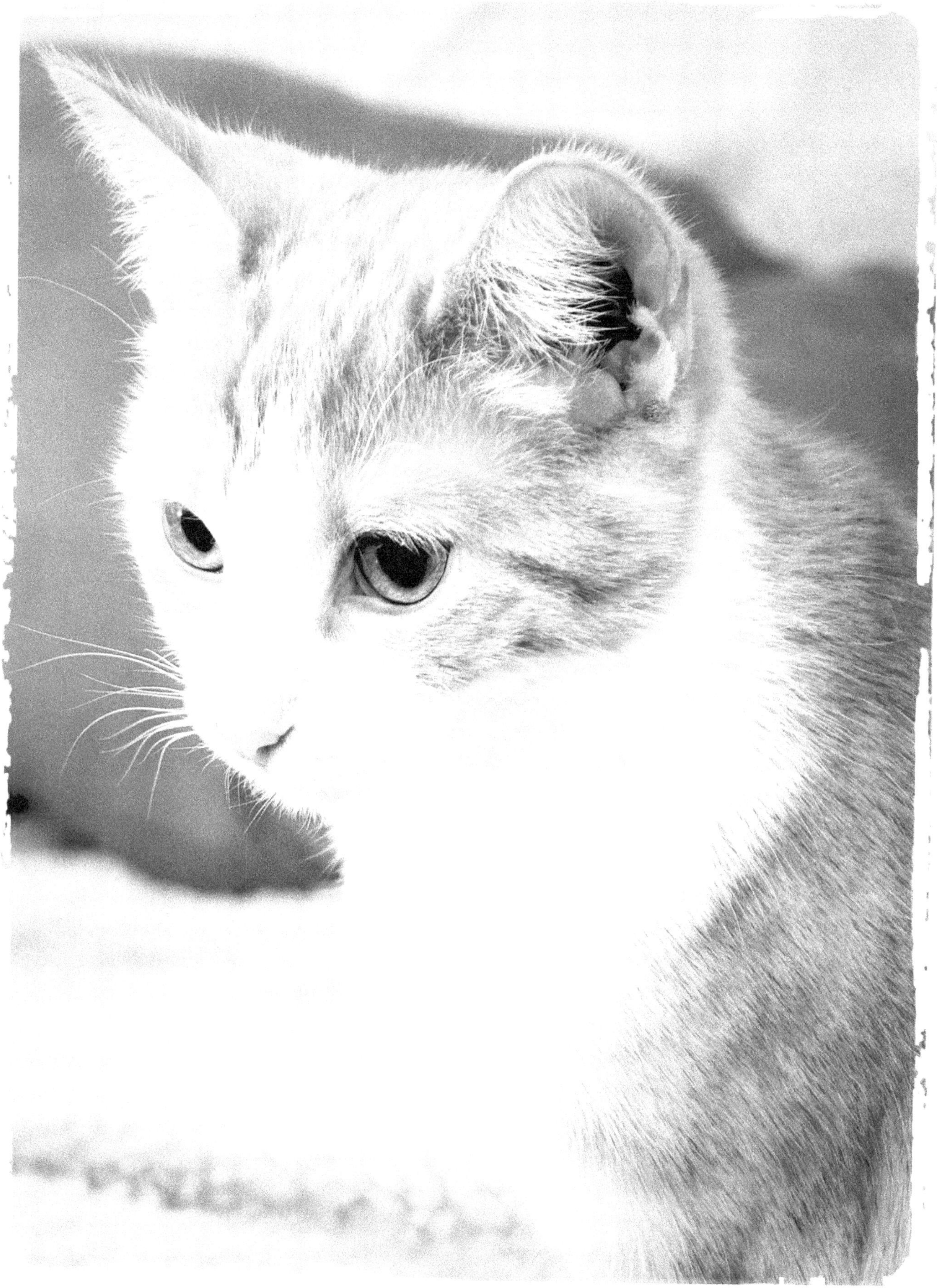

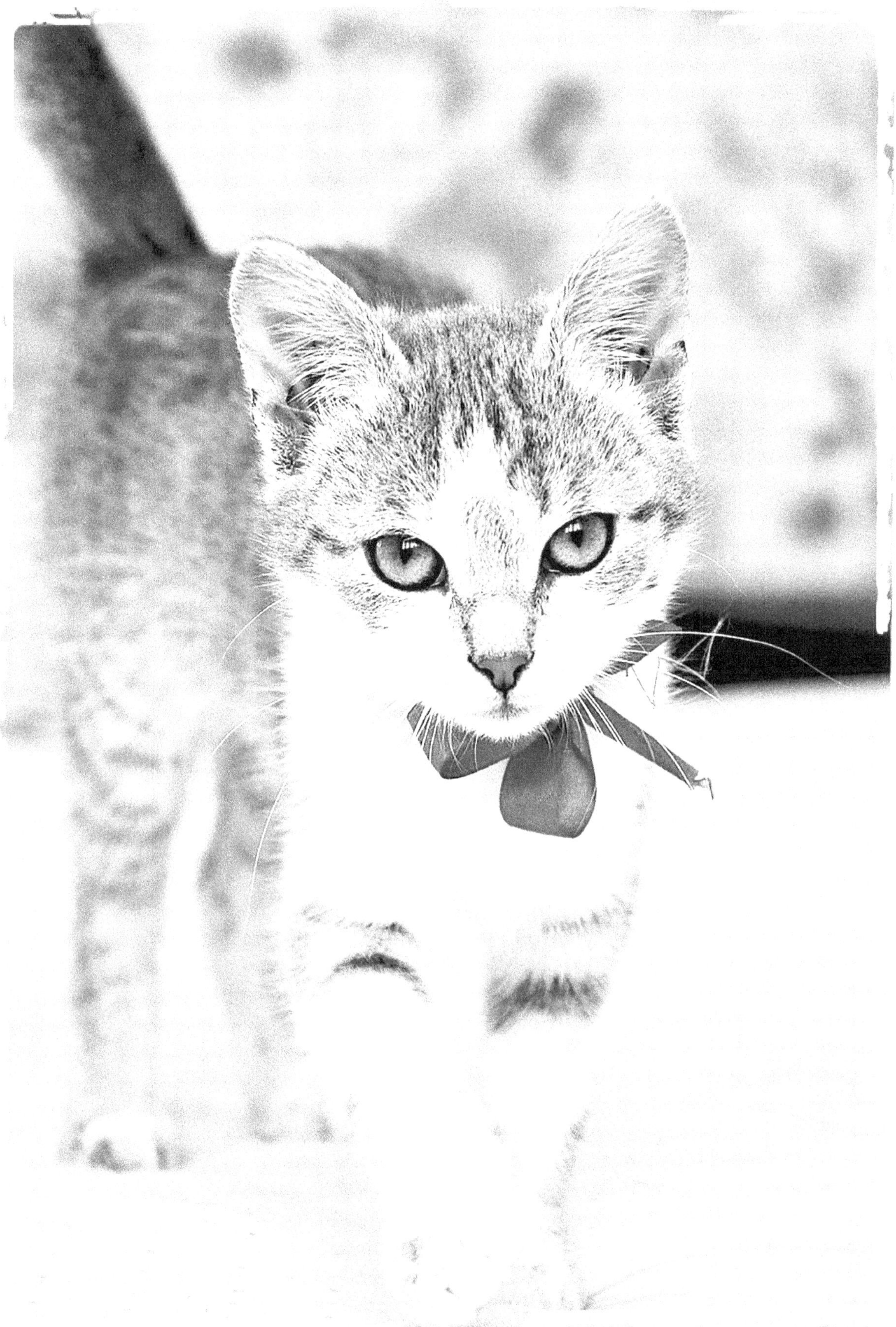

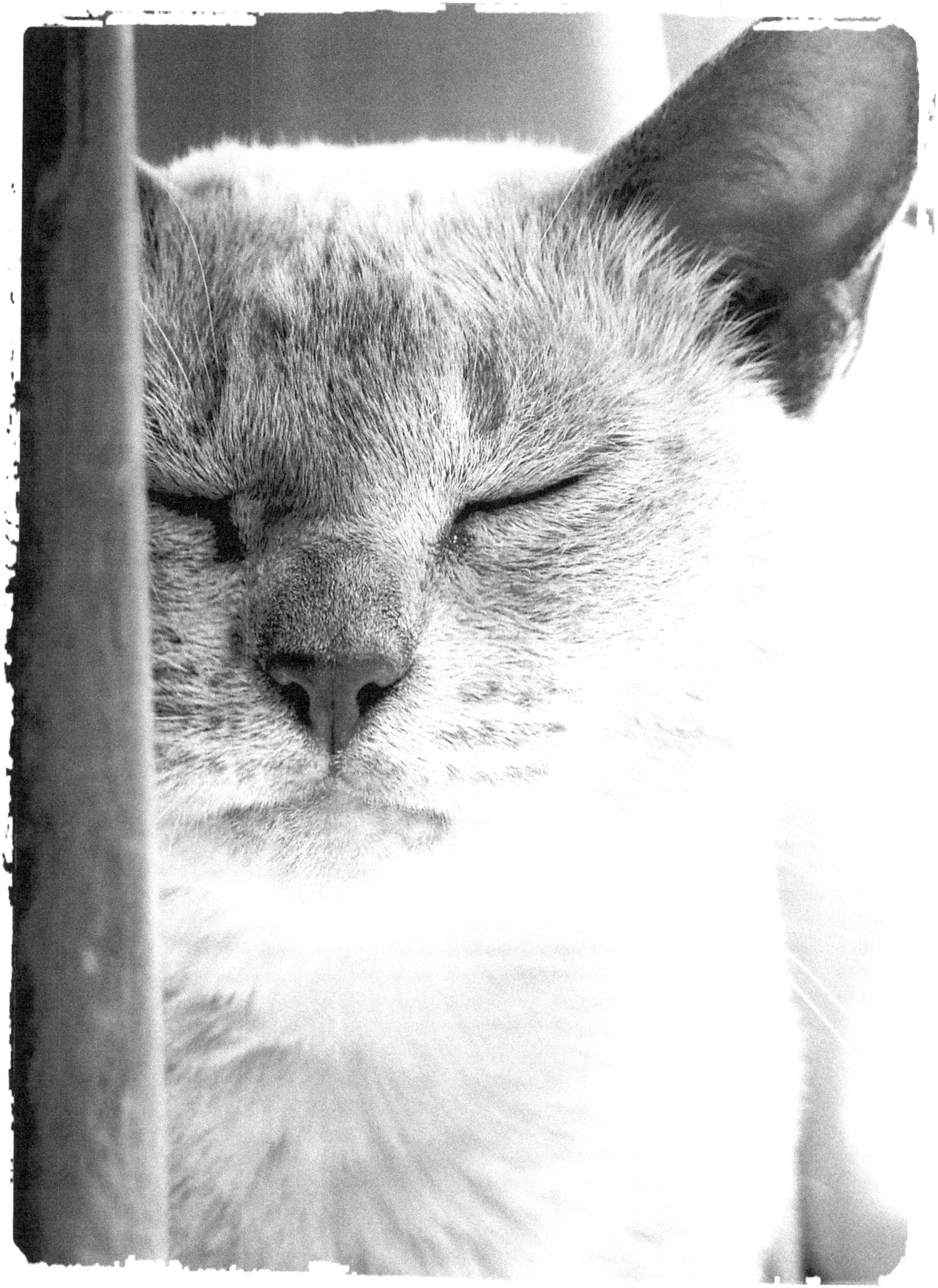

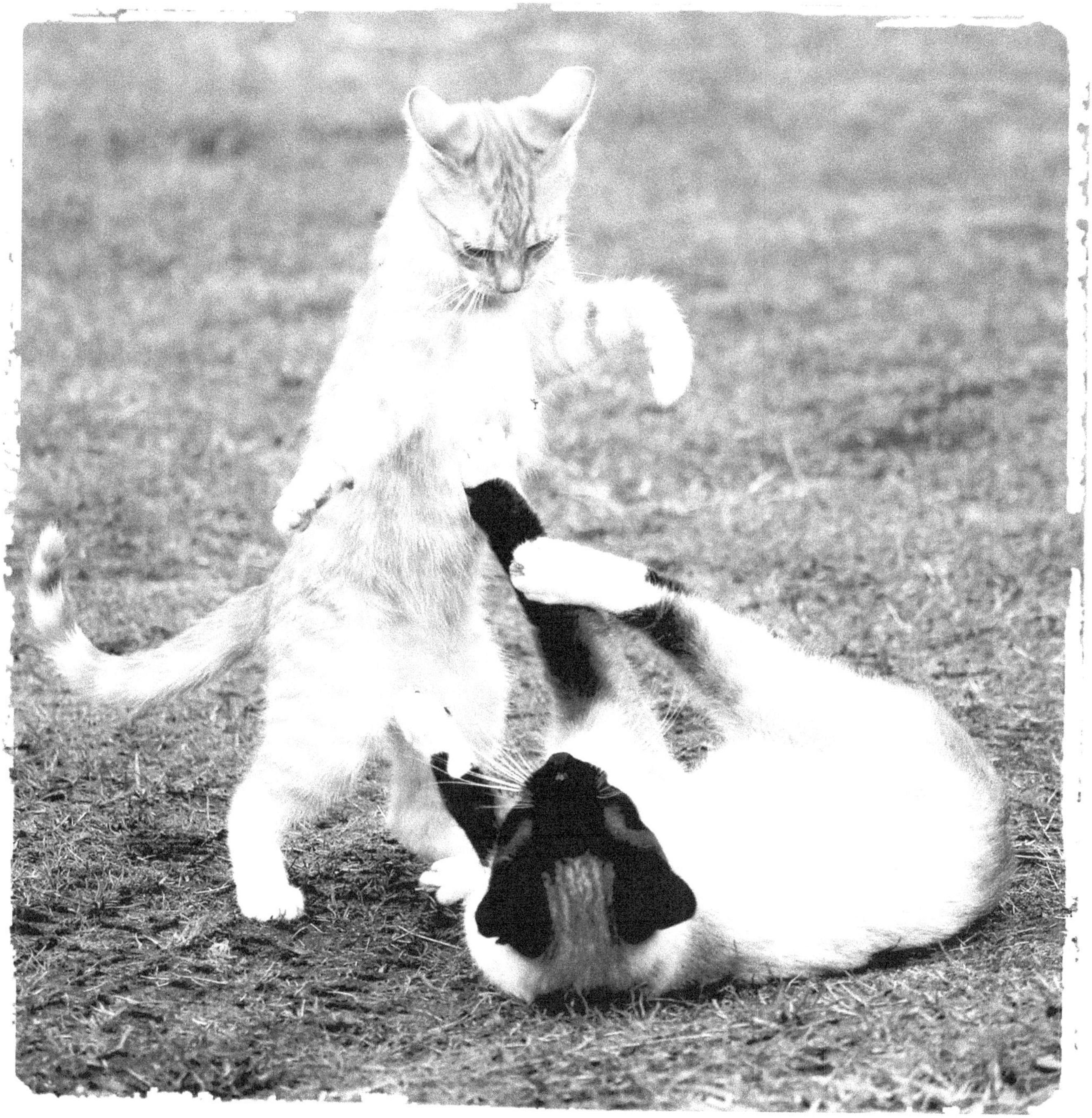

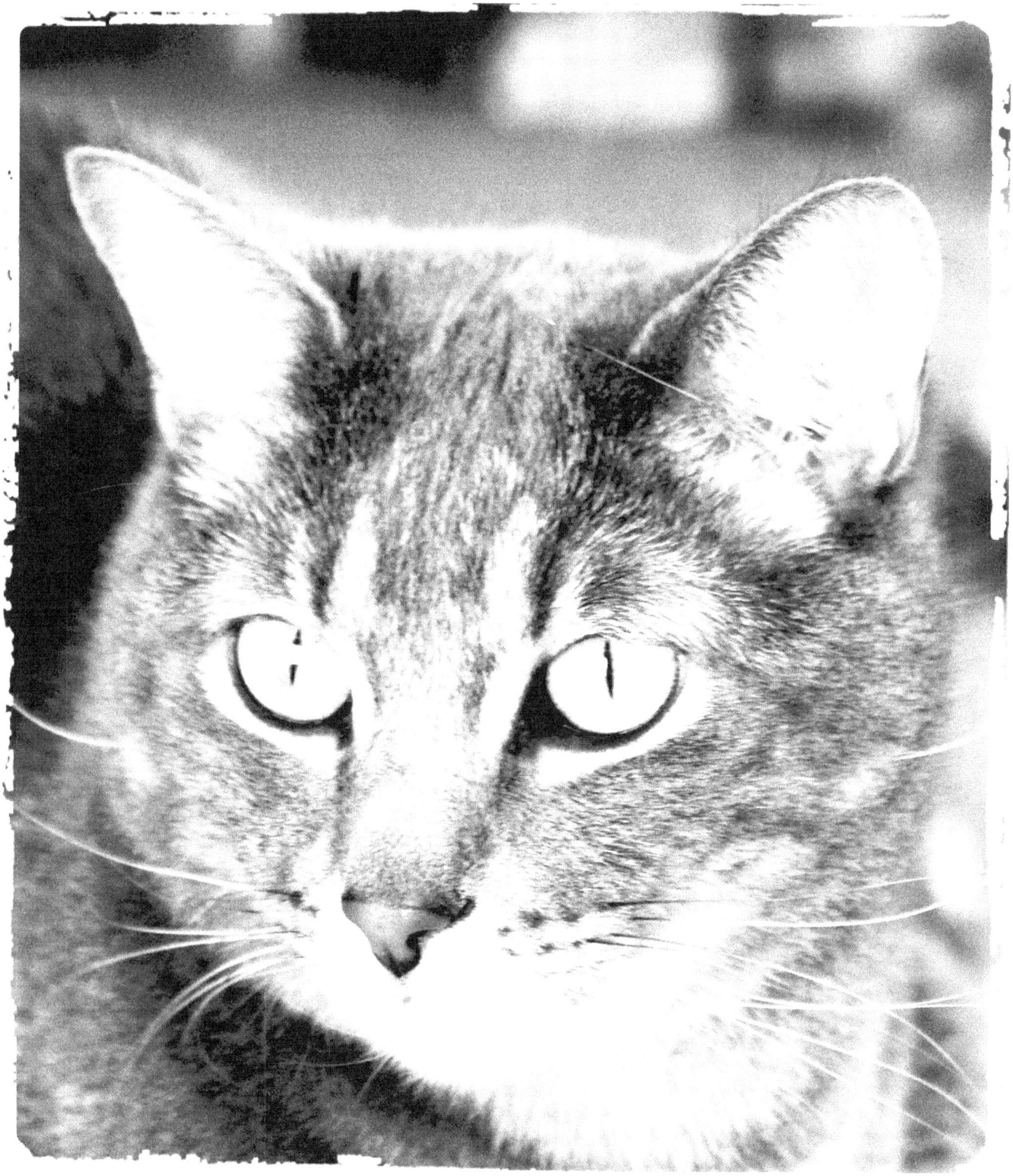

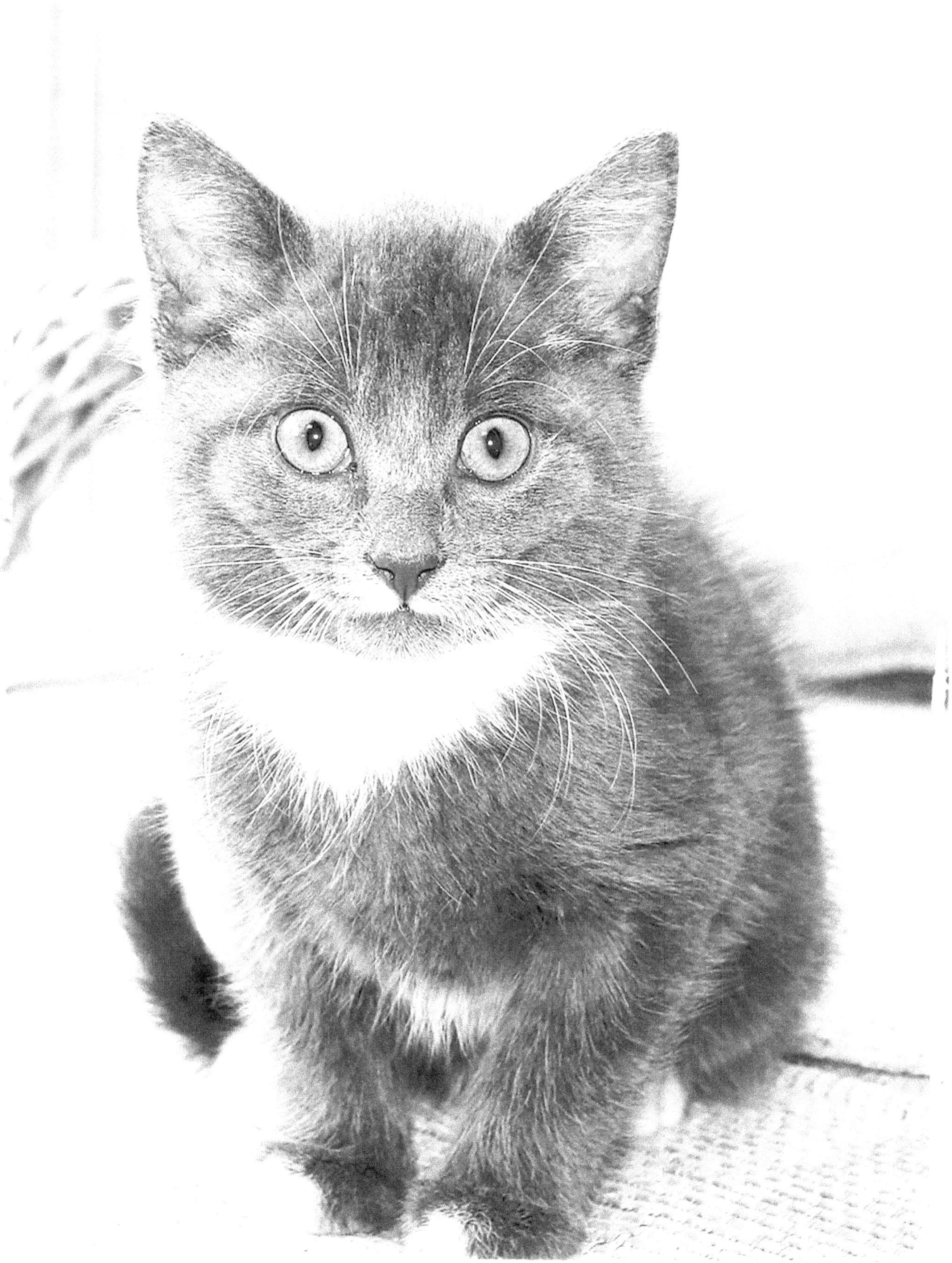

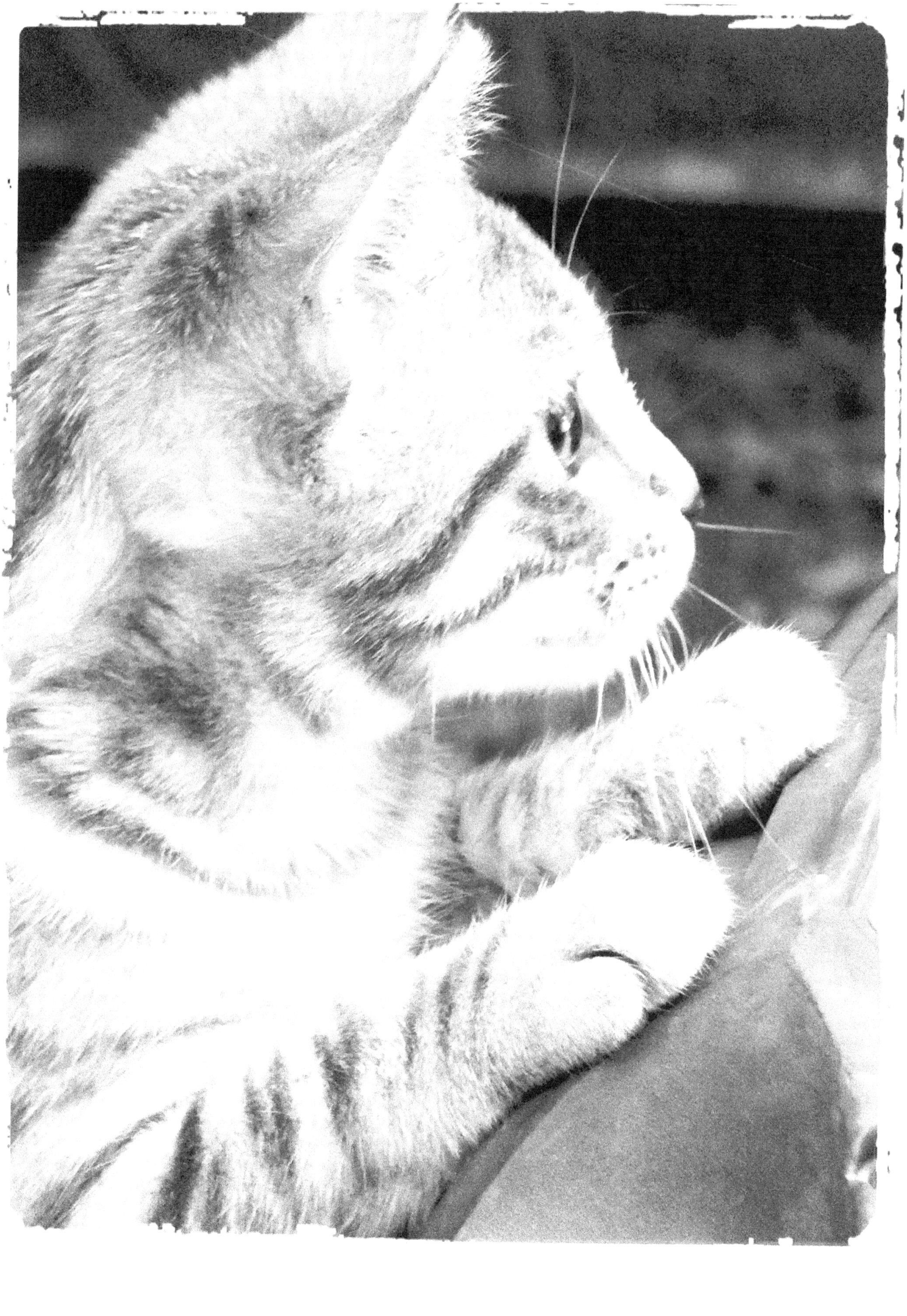

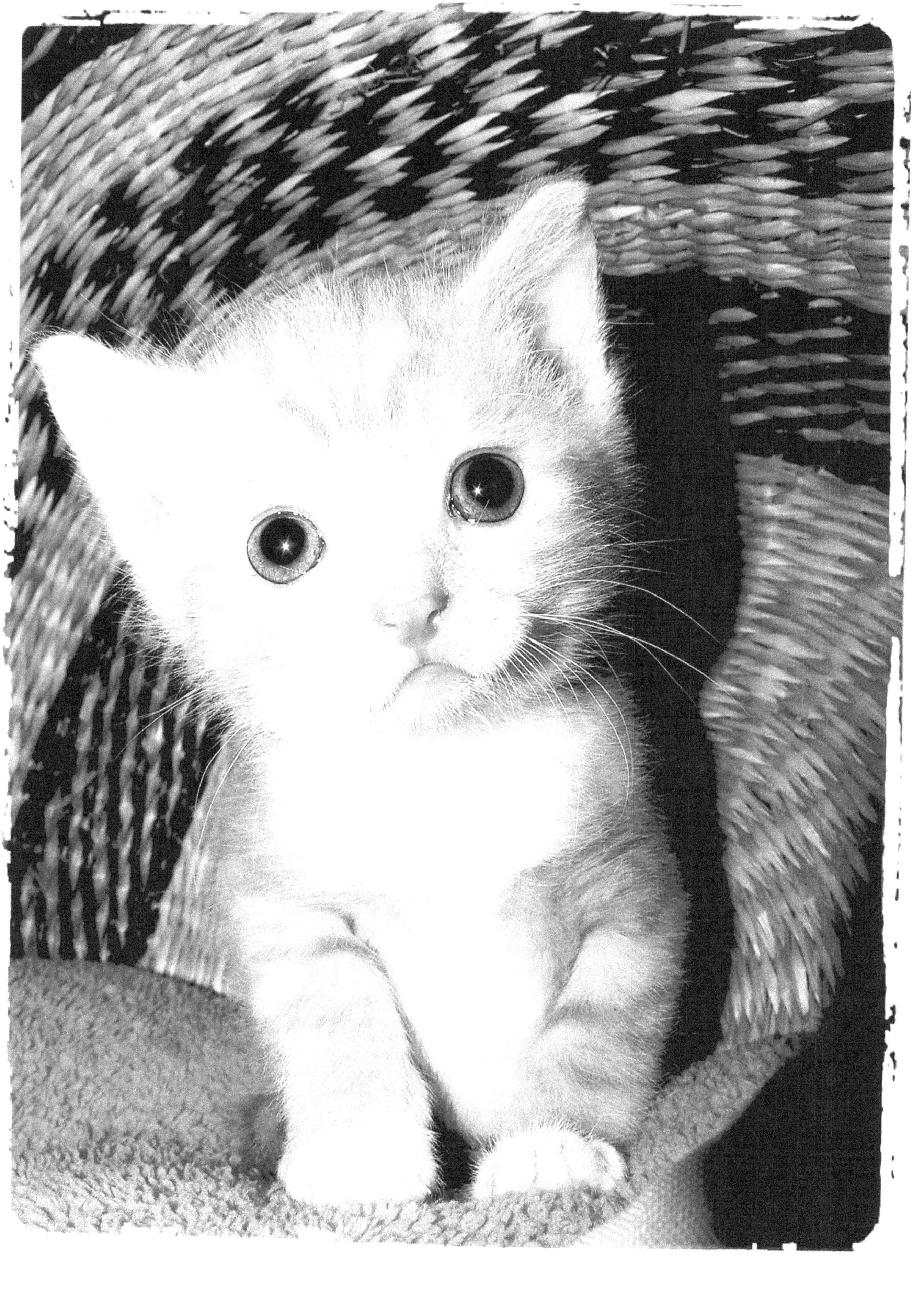

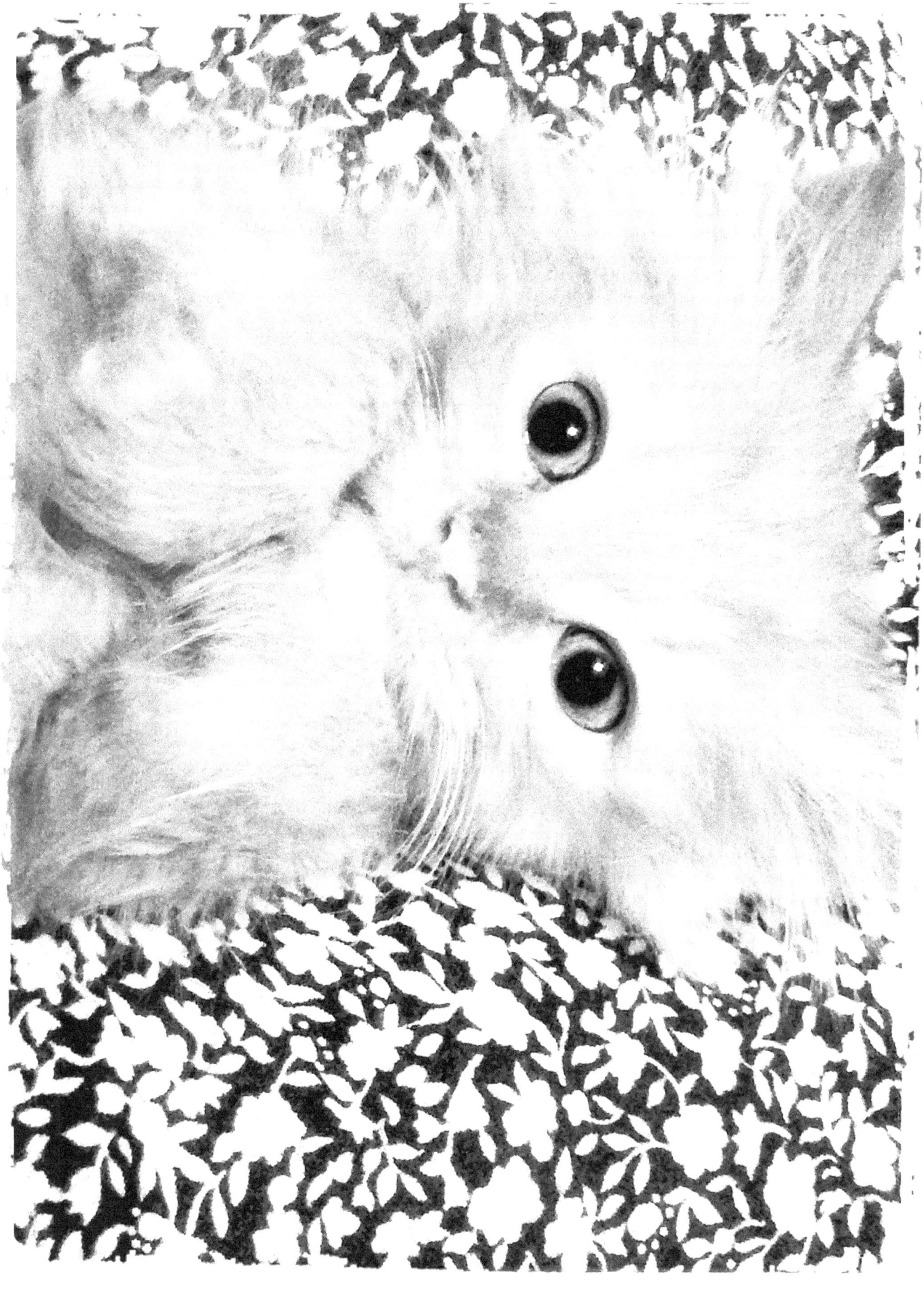

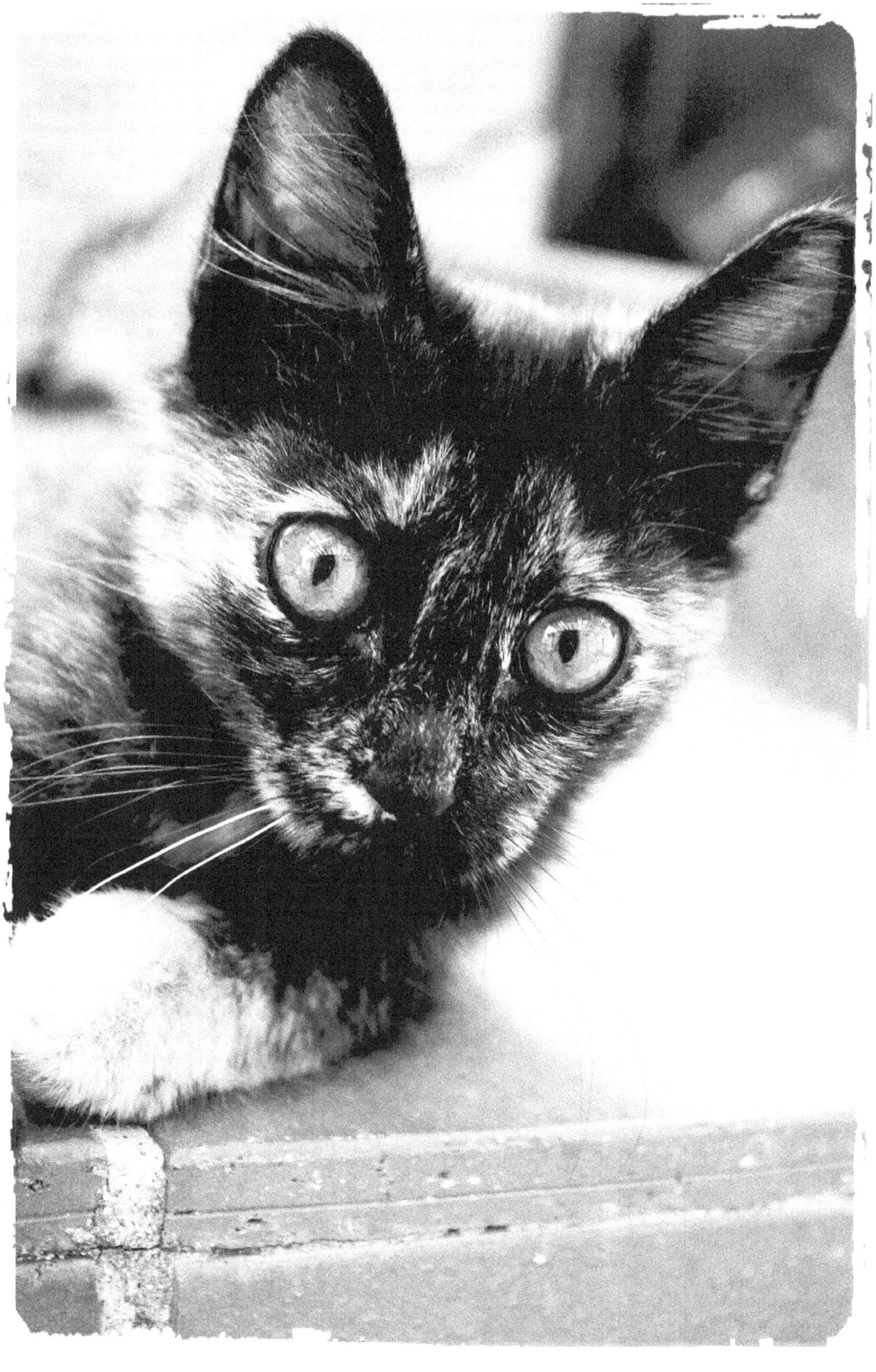

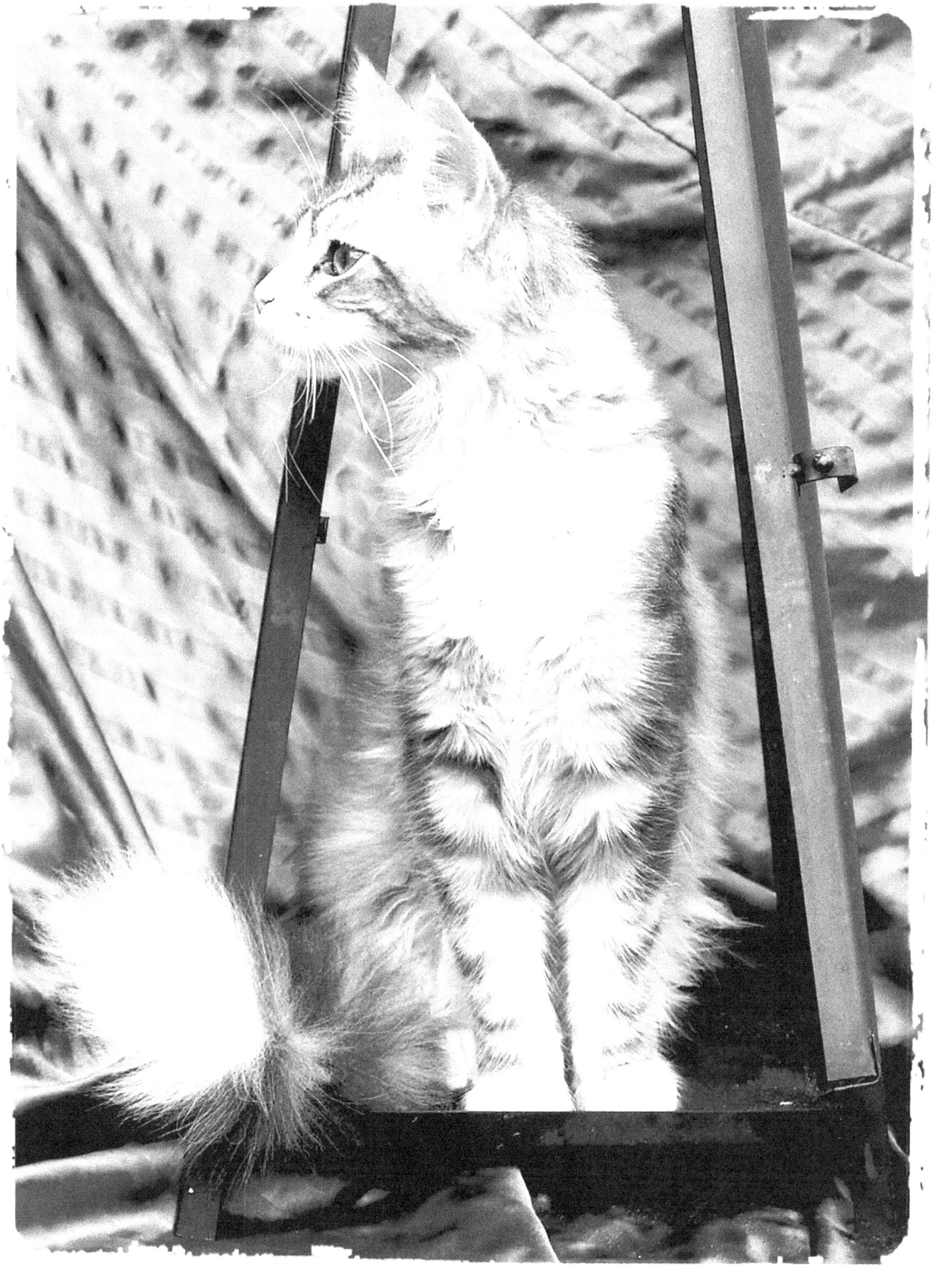

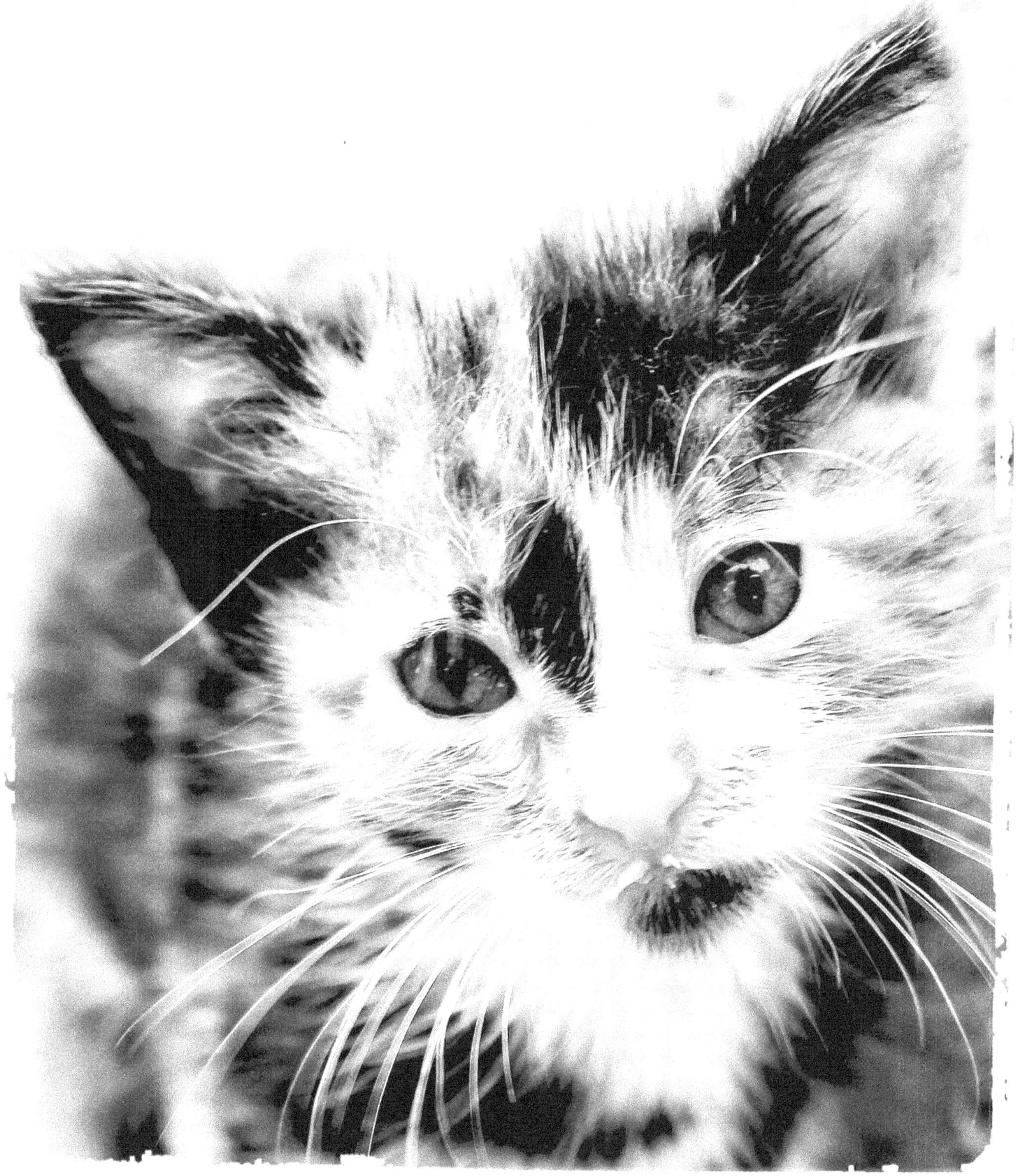

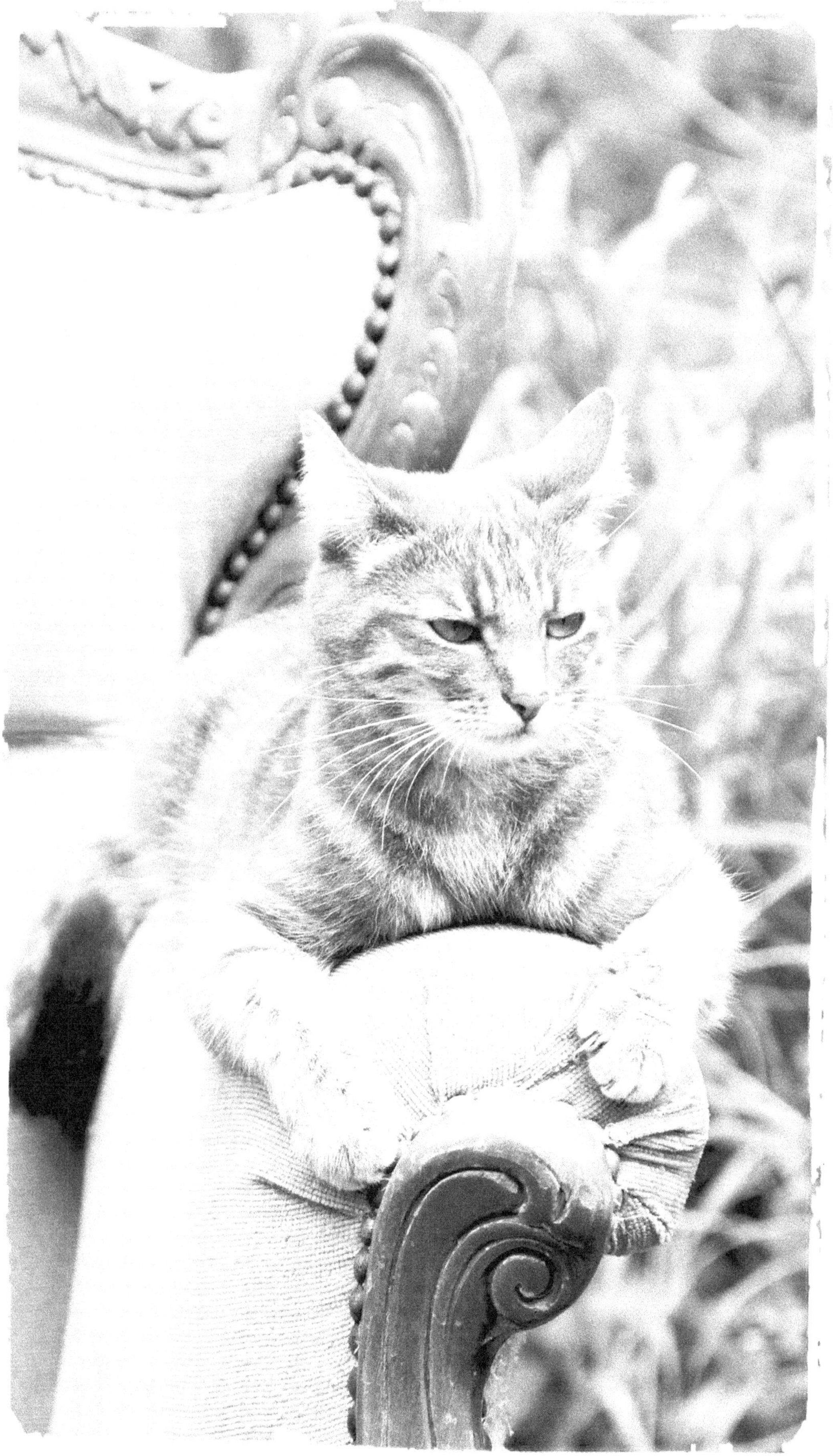

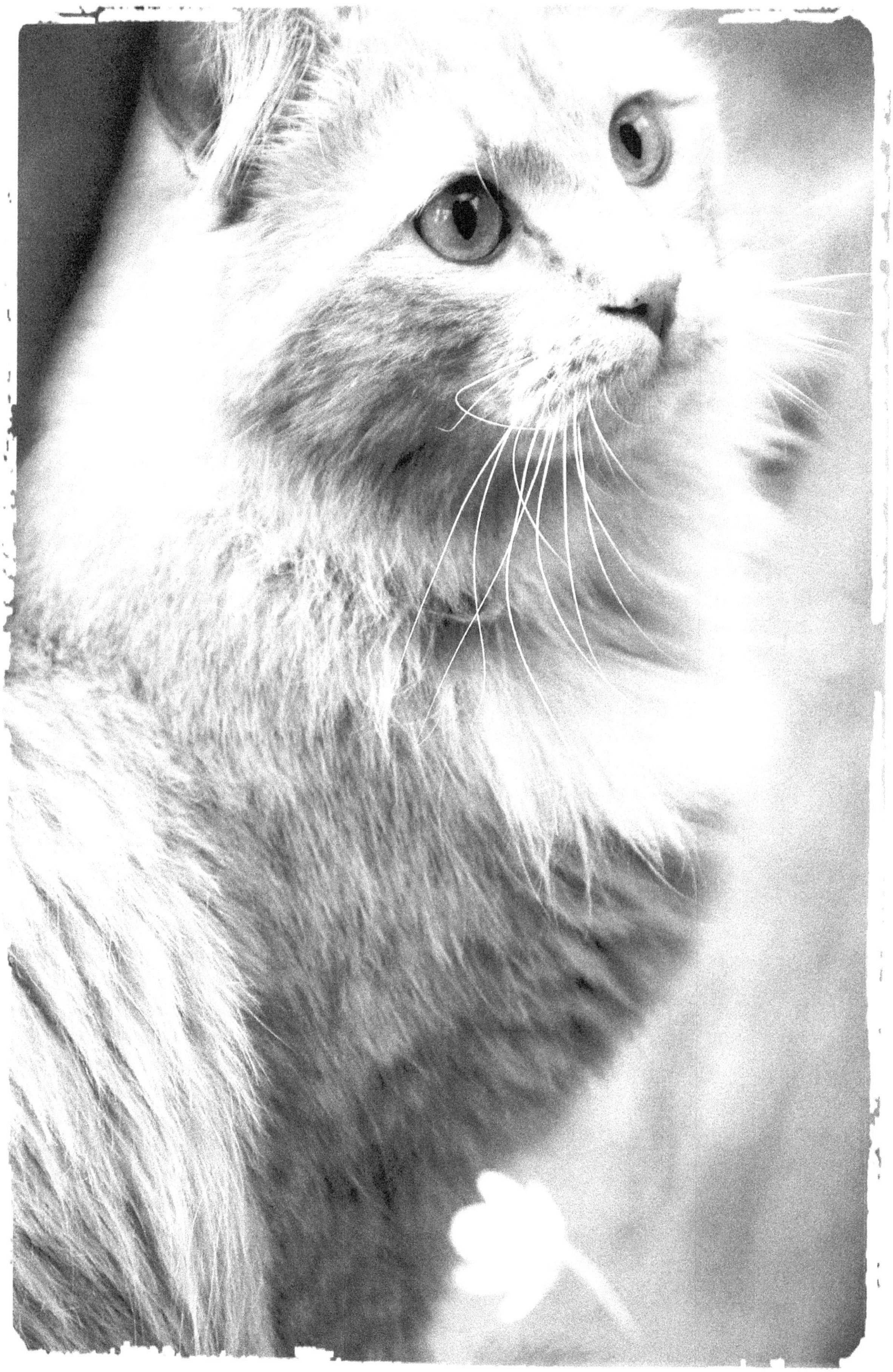

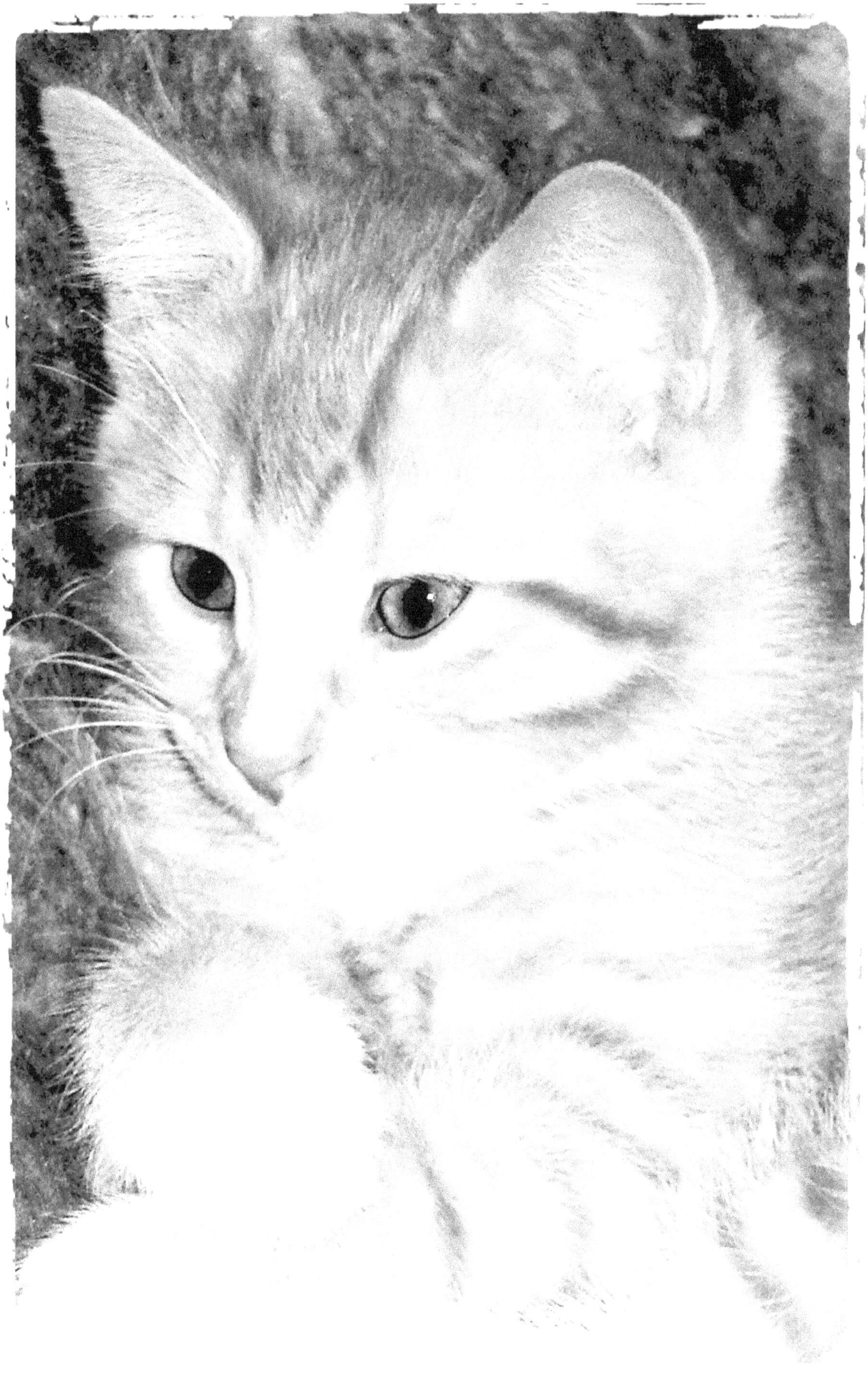

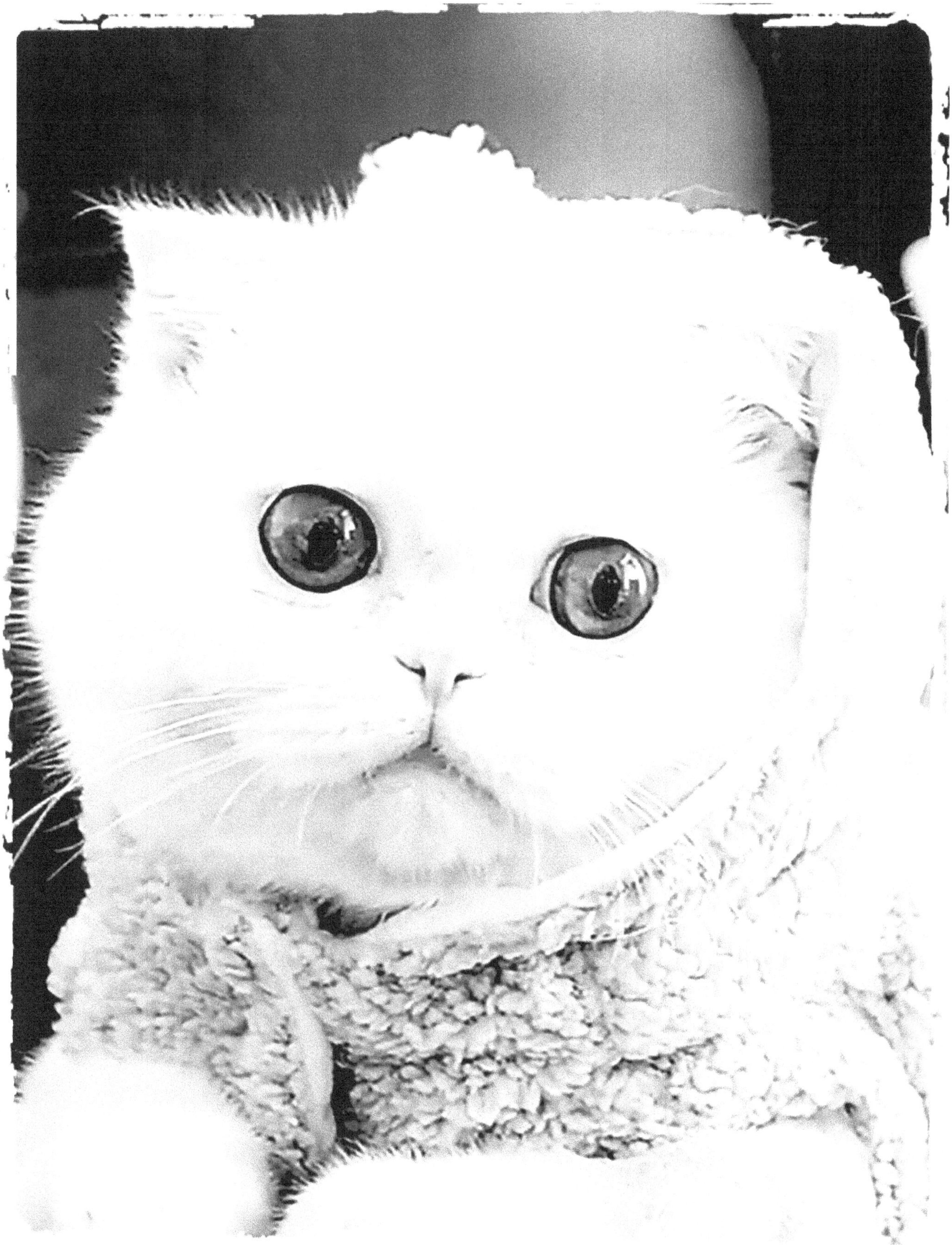

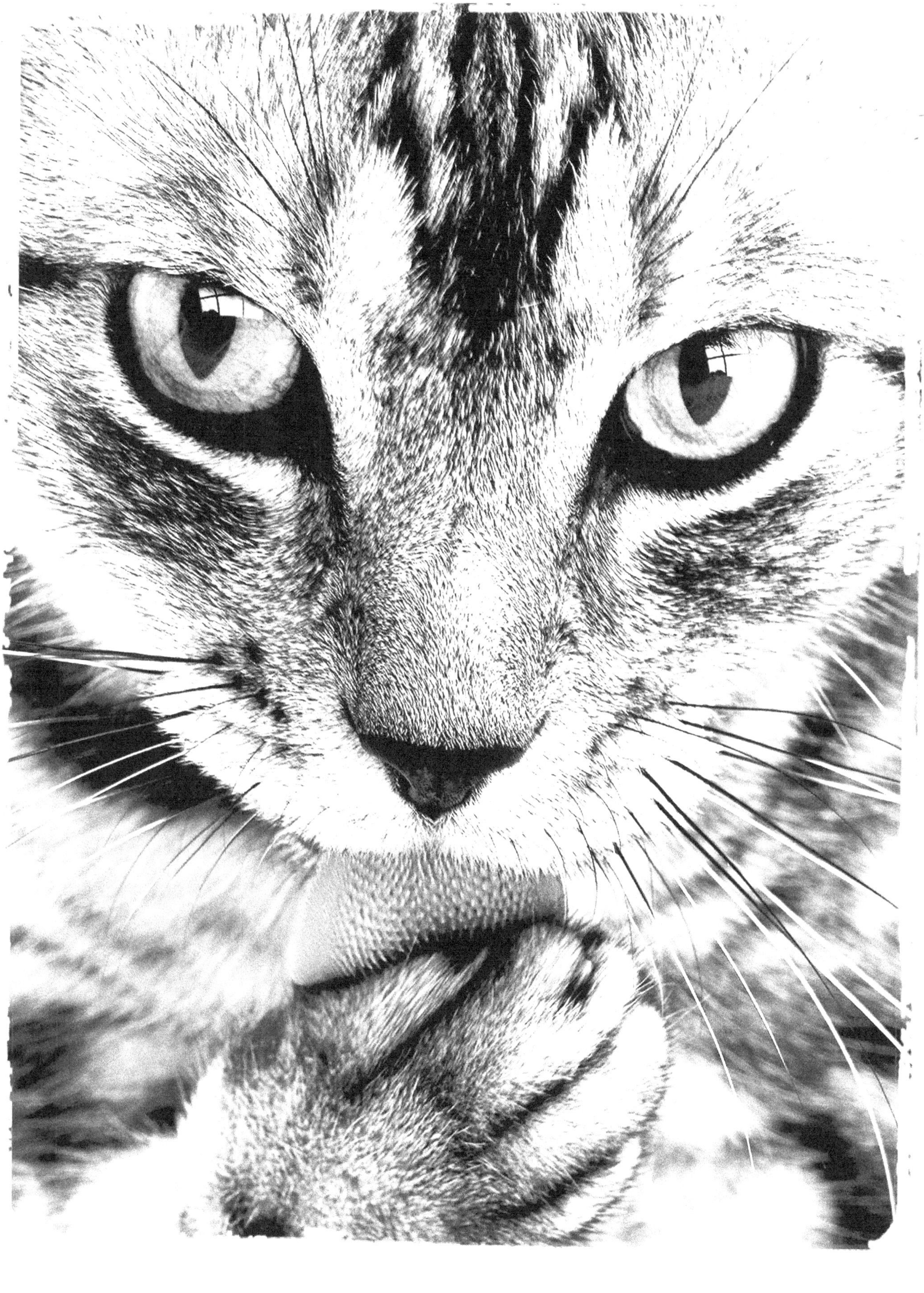

www.ingramcontent.com/pod-product-compliance
Lightning Source LLC
Chambersburg PA
CBHW080541190526
45169CB00007B/2589
* 9 7 8 1 5 3 2 7 6 6 4 2 8 *